First Invite Love In

40 Time-Tested Tools for
Creating a More Compassionate Life

Tana Pesso

with the guidance of

H.H. Penor Rinpoche

WISDOM PUBLICATIONS

Wisdom Publications
199 Elm Street
Somerville MA 02144 USA
www.wisdompubs.org

Library of Congress Cataloging-in-Publication Data
Pesso, Tana.
First invite love in : 40 time-tested tools for creating a more compassionate life / Tana Pesso with the guidance of H.H. Penor Rinpoche.
p. cm.
ISBN 0-86171-285-4 (pbk. : alk. paper)
1. Compassion—Religious aspects—Buddhism. 2. Spiritual life—Buddhism. I. Penor Rinpoche, 1932-2009. II. Title.
BQ4360.P46 2010
294.3'4442—dc22
2009054239

14 13 12 11 10
5 4 3 2 1

Cover design and illustrations by Phil Pascuzzo.
Interior design by Gopa & Ted2, Inc. Set in Palatino Standadrd LT 10/16.
Note: Despite our best diligent research, the source for the typographic ornament used in section openers throughout this book remains unknown to us. If this element is your creation, we will be pleased to offer acknowledgment in future printings.

Advance Praise for

First Invite Love In

"*First Invite Love In* is a clear, practical handbook that will genuinely help anyone who reads it and follows its exercises. It is an especially important guide at a time when so many lack confidence about how to go beyond fear and uncertainty."

Sharon Salzberg, co-founder of the Insight Meditation Society
and author of *Faith* and *Lovingkindness*

"The short exercises presented here will benefit anyone who practices them."

Sakyong Mipham Rinpoche, holder of the Shambhala Buddhist
Lineage and author of *Turning the Mind into an Ally*

"A marvelous, practical book, unlike anything else out there—the ultimate how-to manual for nurturing kindness and compassion. The authors' enthusiasm for compassion is contagious! It's obvious that caring for others is a good idea, and fortunately Tana Pesso and Penor Rinpoche take the reader by the hand and show us how."

—Deborah Schoeberlein, author of *Mindful Teaching and
Teaching Mindfulness*

THE DALAI LAMA

Generally speaking, having a positive mind ultimately brings
us benefit and happiness. According to my own limited
experience, we can change. We can transform ourselves.
Therefore, if we all spend a few minutes every day trying to
develop a positive, compassionate mind, as explained here,
eventually compassion will truly become part of our lives.
It is my prayer that by doing so we shall all contribute to
a genuinely more peaceful and amicable world and to the
lasting happiness of all sentient beings.

For my mother, Diane Boyden-Pesso, who taught me
to have compassion for even the tiniest life forms
on the planet and that differences among people
were to be sought out and celebrated,
not feared.

Table of Contents

INTRODUCTION

How wonderful that you were moved to open this book and have come to this page. Even this one small step is an undeniably good thing, both for you and for the world because you have just acted on an interest in creating a more compassionate life.

Every single action, word, or thought that is motivated by the aspiration to be more kind, to cause less harm, and to create less suffering, sets ripples of goodness in motion that can transform your mind into a sea of tranquility and happiness. What's more, this energy, if reinforced and built upon, can lead to untold positive effects for countless others near and far in both time and place. Again, how wonderful!

Moment by moment, thought by thought, step by step we can transform our minds through time-tested compassion practices, and ultimately create a garden of delight out of any life history or current circumstance, regardless of how traumatic or difficult. There are countless examples of people from all spiritual paths, faiths, and religions who have experienced terrible hardships, or even themselves *created* hardships and suffering for others, who have turned their minds toward love and compassion and found peace and happiness.

My own unshakable confidence in the compassion practices I present in this book is the result of having studied with many great spiritual masters, each of whom possessed a level of kindness and peace of mind that surpassed anything I'd ever personally encountered before. The fact that so many of them had undergone phenomenally painful life experiences made their attainment of contentment, joy, and kindness even more remarkable—and it made their teaching even more compelling.

One might be tempted to imagine that there is something unusual in the makeup of people who can so effectively transform hardship into wisdom and compassion. Moreover, we might imagine whatever that special something is, we ourselves are surely lacking it! Fortunately for us, for you and for me, too, this is not at all the case. Not in the least. In fact, the opposite is true. It is in our very nature to be kind—the very nature of *all* of us, even you, even me; it is part of the very core of our being. No one is born without this essential core of compassion and kindness, and no clumsiness, hardship, or even intentional ill-will can destroy it. Our challenge is to simply *rediscover* this deep compassion and nurture it, to clear away the fog obscuring this primordial reserve of good.

And that's exactly what this book will help you to do.

And I am certain: You *can* succeed!

Even if you have accumulated years and years of conditioning that leads you to act contrary to this kindness, even if you have tried fruitlessly in the past to change only to see yourself fail more vividly even amid and despite your good intentions, even if you have never had so much as a glimpse of being unconditionally accepted and loved—even then you can succeed.

Today is the beginning of a new story for you. A story guaranteed to have a happy ending if only you'll give sufficient time and bring just a little patience, practice, and perseverance. After all, it takes time and practice to change the mind patterns of a lifetime. Yet the truth is that it is entirely within your power and ability—regardless of your past history or your present circumstance—to regain your birthright of a happy, peaceful, and compassionate mind. This book, the one you now hold in your hand, contains a time-tested and proven path that will lead to the happy experience of life that is your heart's desire.

So let us begin this joyful journey!

Some Advice in Using This Book

First and foremost, please be kind and patient with yourself, even merciful, as you work toward developing a more peaceful and compassionate mind. Self-criticism and doubt will likely arise as you work with the practices, but please trust that some good will come of your engagement with them—even if you can't see it right away. And if you *can't* manage to feel that trust, then just be open to the *possibility*—even if you believe it is remote—that some good might come from your efforts.

I suggest you give yourself enough time (and enough practice through repetition) to become completely comfortable and proficient with the ideas and visualizations in each practice before moving on to the next one. But it's also important that you follow your own instincts about how to pace your work with the practices. As long as you come back at some point to take the next step forward in expanding your heart and mind for greater peace and compassion, that is all that matters.

You'll no doubt find that some practices come easily to you whereas others might feel like unfamiliar or even uncomfortable ground. Exercises of this latter type will require revisiting a few times before they really take hold in your mind. Until they do, *please* be patient with yourself and treat yourself kindly.

Visualizations figure prominently in the guided meditations—yet a natural facility to visualize is in no way necessary. Merely *thinking about* each thing that is described is sufficient to help open your heart and mind to greater peace and happiness. You might see it in vivid and detailed Technicolor, or you might have just a vague visual impression in your mind, or you might even "see" nothing at all. It truly doesn't matter in the least. It is entirely enough to just contemplate the meaning of the scene as it is described in the guided meditation.

The practices in this book have one purpose: to train your heart and mind to experience greater peace and compassion. For this to happen, there's no need to increase the power of your concentration or your ability to do visualizations; to begin these practices there's no need whatsoever for your mind to be even the slightest bit different than it already is.

A word of clarification: Don't try to use these exercises to affect or influence people other than yourself or to change anything in the world other than your own habits of mind. Nonetheless, by opening just our own hearts and minds to experience greater peace within and greater compassion for the pain of others, we *do* somehow help the universe itself to relieve both ourselves and others of suffering and to attain greater happiness.

One more thing: Please do try to remember as you work with the visualizations that we do not have to do all the heavy lifting ourselves. Our own role in the cosmic scheme of things is modest: to work steadily and faithfully toward achieving a kinder and more peaceful state of mind within. And this small act alone, through the unknowably and unimaginably interconnected web of causes and conditions that connects all beings in the universe, will of itself serve to uplift, not only ourselves, but all others too.

Do the Exercises in Order and Don't Skip Steps

The order of presentation of the exercises in this book has been designed to slowly build your mental capacity to experience peace and compassion through progressively more subtle and challenging practices. Each practice builds on the preceding ones, so it is best to do them in the order they are presented here. Jumping around may lead you to become needlessly confused or frustrated. In a way, it's just like learning a new language or becoming proficient in a sport or dance. First there is a certain vocabulary of moves or words one needs to learn, the basic building blocks. Then one learns to connect these building blocks in certain sequences. And finally, through practicing these sequences in a useful order one gains the strength and mastery to play well or express oneself fluently.

Likewise, *within* each exercise there are multiple steps presented in a certain order, each containing a discrete element to be visualized or contemplated. Make sure you really take the time to visualize or contemplate *each* element before moving on to the next. You will find this is much easier and more fruitful than reading through the entire exercise and then trying to reconstruct it in your mind.

The opening segment of each exercise is called "First Invite Love In." Since this step is the same for each of the forty exercises, it is presented only once at the beginning of the book. But please know that this step is *crucial* to each exercise, and should *never* be skipped. This is the part of the practice that will provide you with the spiritual and emotional resources to open your heart during the central meditation without feeling drained or anxious. Skipping the first segment would be like exercising without having taken in the nourishment you need to support the expenditure of energy. Your body is surely going to run down, and quickly.

The second segment of each, "Then Send Love Out," contains the compassion practice proper. The final segment of each, "Seal with a Vow and Rejoice," will help you to retain and build upon the new insights and states of mind that you have gained through the guided meditation. Skipping this segment would be like failing to properly protect, label, and store food you had collected. You risk losing both its quality and quantity and may have trouble locating it again when you need it at a later time.

Since the first and last segments remain the same throughout all forty practices, after a while you might be tempted to skip them or give them short shrift. Please don't! Doing so would be doing yourself a disservice in the long run because these two segments will provide you with the wherewithal to stay the course over time until you achieve the results you want. Please also try to give equal weight and attention to each of the three segments of practice.

This format of surrounding the main compassion practice with a means to draw in support at the start and to carefully store any progress made at the end is modeled closely on Eastern meditation techniques that have proved their worth over the millennia for helping people just like us to gain greater peace of mind and happiness. So let's stick with a winning equation and try to give equal weight to all three segments of each guided meditation.

If you wish to repeat a particular practice in order to gain greater comfort and proficiency with it before you move on to the next one in the series, but no longer need the detailed guidance of the full meditation, the back of the book contains a short version of each exercise that you can use as something like a crib sheet, for brief reminders.

Practice Regularly

Establishing a set routine around when and how you work with the practices can also help you to stay the course to complete the entire cycle. If you can, try to work with the practices at the same time and in the same place each day. Writing the time and place of practice in your calendar or posting notes about it in prominent places in your home can help you remember to practice.

Finding a spot of peace and quiet to practice in while you try to attain a peaceful and happy mind can also help. So you might consider making it part of your routine to turn off and away from distractions during your practice time so that you can give your mind your full attention.

Trust Yourself

Although I have thus far expressed what I believe is the time-tested and optimal way to engage these practices, I also want to add this: Should you find that you are more comfortable proceeding with the practices in the book in a different way than suggested, don't hesitate to trust yourself and follow your own course without a second thought.

And above all, please know and keep in mind that any movement toward peace and compassion, however large or small and regardless of gaps in time, stumbles, or setbacks, is cause for celebration.

It is all good and only good!

OPENING AND CLOSING PRACTICES

First Invite Love In

Laying the Foundation for a Compassionate Life

Prior to each day's compassion practice, take a few minutes to mentally dwell in a space of love. Doing so will help you have the spiritual and emotional wherewithal to practice feeling more compassionate toward others without feeling drained. This is a crucially important part of the practice. Please don't skip it!

Detailed Instructions

1. Bring to mind someone with the capacity for profound love, compassion, and peace of mind. This might be a person in your life, someone you know. Perhaps it is your mother or father, an aunt or an uncle, grandparents, a teacher, a good friend. Or it could be a divine, religious, or historical figure that you admire: Mother Teresa; Martin Luther King, Jr.; Siddhartha Gautama, the historical Buddha; the Virgin Mary; God;

Allah; or Jesus. Whoever this person may be, bring them clearly into your mind.

2. Now imagine that person's mind is entirely focused on filling you with a feeling of love and peace. Imagine that their intention is to transfer *their* ability to feel peace, love, compassion, and kindness into your mind. They want to pour their own ability into your mind, into your heart.

3. Think that they do so without any judgment or requirement of you. There is no possibility of criticism. There is no expectation of how quickly or even if you will ever be able to receive this. Imagine that they are completely filled with this feeling of wanting to pour this ability to feel compassion into you, but there is no expectation of whether you will be able to receive this or how you will respond.

4. Imagine also that they have absolutely perfect concentration on maintaining only thoughts of profound love in their minds, and only thoughts of transferring this capacity of profound love into you. So they are not thinking about other people, other problems to solve, anything else.

5. This is completely pure, unconditional love, beaming into you with unbroken concentration for as long as you might need it. Pause and think about that for a moment.

6. Now open your mind to the idea of receiving this love and having your mind become the same as this vast, loving, and peaceful mind that is contemplating you. Just imagine that it is possible.

7. Now mentally ask the envisioned being to help transform your mind into a mind filled with profound love. Imagine saying whatever you might say to ask for this kind of love from this being. Really picture yourself making this request.

8. Then imagine that they respond to your request for help with pleasure and happiness. They are very glad you asked and are delighted to help you. Imagine the words that they would say back to you.

9. Imagine that your spiritual support figure creates a protective sphere around you where nothing disruptive or adverse can enter, harm, or distract you during this meditation.

10. Now form an intention or create an aspiration that *at some point* in time, with practice, your mind will come to mirror the mind of love you have envisioned, your mind will be as loving and compassionate as the mind of the person you are imagining. Say to yourself that you have the intention of developing a mind of greater compassion and kindness.

11. Scan your body and mind and let go of any tension or anxiety you feel as if a fist lets go and opens into a relaxed and open hand. Just let the muscles go. Let the inner tension go. Just let it go.

12. Transfer your attention to what is going on in your mind. Let any thoughts you have slip away as if they were clouds passing in the sky above or bubbles rising and evaporating into the air. Don't follow your thoughts. They are there, but just let them pass by. Don't grab on to any of them and there's no need to push them away, either. Just let them go for a while. It's okay to have them; you can't stop them. But let them rise on up and by.

13. Bring to mind the sum-total of everything you have ever enjoyed, desired, or found pleasing. Then focus on a few things that you especially like—they could be food, experiences, relationships, objects. Then relax your grip on these thoughts and imagine them floating up and out of your mind and eventually disappearing entirely into the sky without a trace. You can let them go for just a little while so we can clear some mental space to contemplate new ways of thinking and feeling.

14. Now that you have taken a few of these thoughts that are pleasing to you, gather more and more of them together. Everything that you have ever really loved, wished you had, or do

have and really enjoy. Just let them rise up and out. Let go of them for a while.

15. In the same way and for the same reason bring to mind your negative thoughts, emotions, and experiences. Think of some things that make you angry, experiences of things that you do not like, any bumpy, muddy, disruptive feelings. Imagine that they drop away from you and your mind is clear of them.

16. Now gather up all of your negative emotions, thoughts, and feelings and things that you really dislike, and imagine that they are magically rendered insubstantial and harmless; imagine they drop away from you in one quick motion, sinking deep into the earth, in a way that doesn't harm the earth and leaving no trace or residue in your mind.

17. Imagine you have a clear mind now. There is nothing you desire. Nothing you are avoiding or disliking. No thoughts that you are running after. No tension gripping in your body.

18. Imagine that all of your pores open to receive the loving mindset of the person or being that you imagine is contemplating you. So they all gently open up. You are quite relaxed. Imagine that your spiritual support figure is protecting you and has made it completely safe to open up like this.

19. Think that you can invite and receive the mindset of the loving being you have envisioned through a point between the eyebrows often called the third eye. Lower your eyes and relax them. Feel the area between your eyebrows gently opening. Then shift your point of perception as if you could see through this window between your eyebrows. You can see the loving being who is contemplating you and who has the intention and the wish to pour their ability to have a compassionate and peaceful and kind mindset into your mind. Imagine that this third eye is especially designed to see and receive peaceful loving thoughts and energy.

20. See the loving being who is contemplating you with unbroken perfect concentration. Experience their profound love and compassion for you with no expectation. You can see this being through this third eye; you have opened all the pores in your body and can receive this loving being's mindset into yourself in this way.

21. Don't strain to maintain this visualization. Don't strain to look or use any effort in any way to actively draw anything into yourself. Just relax and trust. Open yourself up.

22. Perceive the being and allow yourself to receive.

23. Let your mind become one and the same with the loving and peaceful presence you have envisioned.

As you go through the central compassion practice, imagine that the spiritual being you have envisioned is doing a high-level version of it in the most perfect, effortless, and serene manner as a way to support you. Imagine that they pour a never-ending stream of spiritual support into you so that you will have all the emotional and spiritual resources you need to do these mental exercises well and without feeling drained in any way.

 SHORT FORM

Bring to mind your spiritual support figure. Feel their unconditional love beaming into you with perfect concentration for as long as you need. Ask for their help in transforming your mind and see them respond joyfully and happy to help. Aspire to a mind of greater compassion and kindness. Clear your mind and body of distraction, tension, desire, and aversion. Shift your point of perception to your third eye and imagine that you can see and receive your spiritual support figure's state of mind through that portal. Think that your spiritual support figure performs a high-level version of whatever compassion practice you are following, in order to support you.

Seal with a Vow and Rejoice
Tools for Sustaining Compassion

This practice will enhance your retention of any advances you have made in your ability to cultivate and sustain a peaceful and compassionate state of mind. I suggest you use this short meditation at the *end* of each of the main compassion practices in the book.

1. Bring your spiritual support figure clearly into the forefront of your mind.

2. Imagine that this being is unconditionally happy that you have taken this step toward creating a mind capable of greater peace, happiness, and compassion.

3. Make a vow to them and to yourself that you will remember, protect, and further what you have just learned about opening your heart and mind to experience greater peace and compassion.

4. See them swell with feelings of loving support for you and imagine that they transform into a thumb-sized figure that descends down through a channel from the top of your head to rest in a beautiful flower made of light and energy located at your heart center.

5. Next imagine that all the positive, peaceful, and compassionate thoughts that were stimulated by this guided meditation are represented by a small ball of light the size of a pea that also comes to rest in the center of the flower.

6. Imagine that the petals of the flower close up to store it.

7. Think that the pores in your body that had been open to receive the support of the envisioned spiritual being now close up again and return to their natural state.

8. Be kind to yourself and patient with any self-doubt or criticism about the way you engaged with this guided meditation. Rest easy in the knowledge that some good surely came of it, and that is cause for rejoicing without reservation.

 ## Short Form

Imagine your spiritual support figure is pleased with your compassion practice. Vow to continue your efforts. Visualize your support figure and all the compassionate thoughts you generated transforming into two pea-sized balls of light. Imagine these two balls coming down from the crown of your head to rest in a flower of light at your heart center. Imagine the petals closing around them to store and protect them. Be kind and patient with yourself.

THEN SEND LOVE OUT

Tools for Creating a Compassionate Life

Thinking of Friends as Kind Mothers

THIS PRACTICE WILL HELP YOU:

▶ Increase trust of others by creating a sense of kinship.

▶ Increase love for others by creating a sense of gratitude.

▶ Reduce feelings of divisiveness and "us vs. them."

STEP ONE: Use the "First Invite Love In" meditation on page 15 before you begin this guided meditation.

STEP TWO: Please follow the instructions below for the central part of this compassion practice.

STEP THREE: Use the "Seal with a Vow and Rejoice" meditation on page 22 when you conclude this guided meditation.

1. First bring to mind a friend or someone you like very much. Your relationship with this person doesn't have to be perfect but it should be

one about which you have at least *some* good feelings. It may not even be someone you know personally. This person could be a man or a woman. It doesn't matter. The person could be a family member, friend, work colleague, someone from the past, or a passing acquaintance. Whoever it is, just think about this person and bring them into the forefront of your mind.

2. The next thing you are going to do is willingly suspend disbelief and just *pretend* for the sake of this exercise that there is such a thing as a past life. You don't have to actually believe in past lives in order to follow this meditation. We are just playing with the ability of your mind to imagine things. With that in mind, imagine that in one of your past lives this person had been the most loving and caring mother possible to you.

It's important to note that in this meditation you are not visualizing the person as you know them now. It is the *essence* of this person in an (imaginary) past life where they were an entirely different person, and they were the ultimate, perfect, loving mother to you. Imagine the most ideal, loving, wonderful mother and then think that the essence of that perfect mother is actually this person you are thinking of from this life. We're imagining that they are just in a different form, between the past life and this one, but the essence is the same. Similarly, it's also important to note that this imagined perfect mother in a past life is also *not* the same as your experience of *your mother in this life*. Imagine that in a past life you had just the most terrific, completely flawless, perfectly loving and caring mother.

3. With that in mind, try to vividly imagine this mother as she is making every sacrifice for you, doing everything she can at every step and stage in your life to make sure that nothing terrible could ever happen to you. For example, you might imagine that you are about to stumble in front of a wagon and she scoops you up. Or as a baby who doesn't know better, you are going to put your hand in a fire, and she pulls it away. Or somebody is mean to you, and she makes that person stop it. Imagine times in your past life when you are sad, and she comforts you. Or see all the times when you are hungry, and she is making meals for you. You are imagining all the different ways that this mother in a past life is so loving and kind to you. Feel how much she cares for you. You can think about different things she might have done for you at different stages in this past life. Experience them as if they are happening to you at that age in your life in real time.

4. Then think if you were that child in a past life receiving so much kind love and caring how grateful you would have been to her. Think how grateful you would have been when this person was taking such kind care of you when you were a child. Imagine this terrifically loving relationship where you

are being showered with love and care from this mother, and let feelings of gratitude rise up in you. See yourself responding with words to her, such as "Thank you, Mommy! Thank you." Just feel how grateful you would be.

5. Now you are going to try this process again thinking about a different person you like or who you think cares about you. Try the whole thing all over again in your mind. Take the essence of that person. Suspending disbelief, imagine that you are in another lifetime, and that in that past life this person was a perfectly wonderful, loving, and kind mother for you. Remember, they don't have the face or personality they do now. They are in the mode and the being of a perfect, perfect mother.

6. See all the kind things they are doing for you. Imagine all this kindness and care showering on you.

7. Imagine how loved and how grateful you'd feel as a result. Experience this feeling of gratitude. Let your gratitude rise up in you and come back to this mother. You'd want to do anything for her because she had been so kind to you. See the love coming into you and evoking a response of love and gratitude in you toward your mother.

8. If you can, throughout your day (or throughout the coming week), try this visualization out repeatedly by thinking of other people with whom you come in contact who seem kind to you. Look at them and think, "What if that person in a past life had been my mother and had been so incredibly kind to me? Boy, I would have been so grateful!"

I hope that this starts some wheels turning in your mind and starts your heart opening and that the compassion-generating dynamic is starting to move within you.

 ## SHORT FORM

Think about a friend or someone you like very much. Imagine that in a past life this person had been the most loving and caring mother to you conceivable. Imagine that this person made every sacrifice possible to shield you from danger, comfort you in sadness, and attend to your every need. Then think about how grateful you would have been to this person when they were taking such kind care of you when you were a child. Now try this in your mind as much as possible, thinking about other people you like or consider as friends.

Breathe In with Compassion, Breathe Out with Loving-Kindness (Part 1)

THIS PRACTICE WILL HELP YOU:

▸ Increase awareness of the suffering of others and aspiration to relieve them of that suffering.

▸ Increase feelings of loving-kindness toward others and an aspiration to contribute to their happiness in life.

▸ Create an association in your mind between a basic life function (breathing) and feelings of compassion and loving-kindness.

STEP ONE: Use the "First Invite Love In" meditation on page 15 before you begin this guided meditation.

STEP TWO: Please follow the instructions below for the central part of this compassion practice.

STEP THREE: Use the "Seal with a Vow and Rejoice" meditation on page 22 when you conclude this guided meditation.

1. Imagine that you have the power and the ability to relieve all the misery and suffering of all living beings on the planet by drawing it into you with your breath. You might imagine it as black smoke or mist or soot on all the suffering beings that, as you inhale, all draws into you and off of them. A crucial part of this practice is to clearly visualize that drawing in the suffering of others doesn't burden you in any way. So you don't need to worry about taking on the burdens of the world and being crushed by them. What we are imagining is that you can take burdens off of everyone else. You can relieve them of their pain and misery and suffering, and it comes right up and off of them. You are drawing it into yourself, but it doesn't crush you or burden you. You are just relieving them. Inside you the suffering becomes insubstantial and dissolves entirely.

2. Take a moment to first be aware of suffering of all kinds: mental suffering, physical suffering, spiritual suffering, pain, hunger, hurt, disappointment, death, and illness that occurs all around the world for people and animals in all stages of their lives. See it.

3. Imagine that you are able to draw all of that off of them. It is lifting off, streaming off of them, and you are pulling it into

yourself. Again, this doesn't burden you or crush you or hurt you or lessen your lifespan or your happiness in any way. You are just able to pull it all off of them and into you, where it dissolves entirely.

4. Now imagine that you have built up a store of peace and happiness within you. It is like a storehouse for grains, but it contains all of the good things and small moments of kindness that you have done in this life.

5. Imagine that you are able to send out feelings of peace and happiness to all living beings from that storehouse by breathing it out of you.

6. See those positive feelings infusing them with a brilliant white light as you breathe out. As you do this, know that it doesn't in any way take away from your own peace and happiness. Think that the more that you share, the greater will be your own storehouse of peace and happiness. You don't have to protect yourself by hoarding it. You can send it out to everyone.

7. Imagine people lighting up with the brilliant white light you are sending out by exhaling and experiencing peace and happiness. As you exhale, this wonderful peace and happiness in a white light extends out to all living beings, filling them

with peace and happiness. Yet even as you do this, it does not deplete you in any way; know clearly that your positive energy is limitless.

8. Do this part again: First become aware of all the pain, unhappiness, and suffering of all the living beings across the planet. Then repeat steps 3–7 at least three more times.

 ## SHORT FORM

Imagine that you have the power to relieve all the misery and suffering of all living beings by first breathing it like harmless black smoke or mist into yourself. Then imagine that from your store of merit and virtue, built up from the good things you have done and thought during your life, you send out peace and happiness to all living beings by infusing them with inexhaustible brilliant white light as you breathe out. Repeat this as many times as possible.

3

Widening the Heart to Embrace the World with Loving-Kindness and Rejoicing

THIS PRACTICE WILL HELP YOU:

▸ Increase feelings of loving-kindness for others.

▸ Widen the heart to embrace the greatest number of people possible.

▸ Overcome or reduce the view of life as a zero-sum game in which all success comes at the expense of someone else's failure.

▸ Increase the ability to rejoice in the happiness of others.

STEP ONE: Use the "First Invite Love In" meditation on page 15 before you begin this guided meditation.

STEP TWO: Please follow the instructions below for the central part of this compassion practice.

STEP THREE: Use the "Seal with a Vow and Rejoice" meditation on page 22 when you conclude this guided meditation.

1. Bring to mind someone that you care deeply about. Think about someone that you like a great deal and for whom you have a lot of warm feelings. This would be the kind of person for whom you would wish all the best things in the world would happen. Bring this person clearly into the forefront of your mind.

2. Then think about what you know of the kind of wonderful things that this person actually wishes or hopes or might likely wish or hope could happen in their lives. Also, think about the positive things that you wish or hope would and could happen to this person.

3. Next imagine that these things actually come about in this person's life. See the picture of the person that you have in mind and then see these wonderful things happening to them.

4. Then imagine how happy they would be. See them become very happy, delighted, pleased, relieved, relaxed, and fulfilled. See them smiling with happiness and feeling at peace and relaxed. Imagine them feeling blessed because all these wonderful things have happened in their life. That's a nice picture.

5. Now stretch this a little bit further. Think of your family members. Bring them to mind as a group. Remember that this

is all happening just within your mind. You don't have to exert yourself to do the impossible or some kind of magic. It's not as if we are trying to make this happen in the real world. We are just imagining this happening in the arena of our own minds.

6. See your family members in your mind and imagine that everything that they would like to have happen in their lives actually comes about. Do this to the best of your ability even if you have negative feelings or difficult relationships with some or all of your family.

7. Then see them light up with happiness, delight, fulfillment, and peace because all these wonderful things have happened. Just see that for a moment . . . *Wonderful!*

8. Now think of all your friends, together and as a group. All your friends are in the forefront of your mind.

9. Imagine that a shower of blessings falls upon them and everything that they would hope would happen in their lives actually comes about. Imagine this or think about this with as much detail as you can.

10. See all your friends light up with happiness, delight, and fulfillment. Feel how happy they feel because everything that

they had hoped for—all their cherished dreams of a good life—has come about. One great thing after another happens to them, making their lives wonderful in all the ways that they would wish.

11. Now take it a bit further. Think about the *entire neighborhood* where you live. See five hundred people or a thousand people in your mind. For all of these people envision that suddenly there is a cloud of happiness and shower of blessings raining down on your neighborhood. Everybody in the neighborhood has the best of luck. Wonderful things come their ways.

12. Visualize that all these people are delighted. See them all light up with happiness and feel how happy they all are. Imagine that the whole neighborhood lights up with relief, happiness, and expansive feelings.

13. Next stretch your visualization of this to encompass the entire *state* where you live. See one big happy state where everything wonderful happens for all people. See them all being delighted by it.

14. Then stretch this scenario out across your country. See everyone in the entire *country* having good fortune and being delighted by it.

15. Now stretch this imagery in your mind to include the entire world. In the theater of your own mind, imagine good luck, good fortune, and all kinds of lovely things happening to everyone. It is a world of delight, a world of happiness.

Remember, you aren't *actually* trying to somehow bless the whole world with your own personal powers. All the thoughts and images that you've had of the world have only been in your mind and imagination. This isn't a prayer or anything other than a mental exercise within the confines of your own mind.

 ## Short Form

Imagine all the wonderful things you hope will happen in the life of someone you care deeply about. Imagine their happiness when these things take place. Next imagine that this happens to every person in your family. Then to all of your friends. Then to everyone in your neighborhood, your state, your country, and ultimately to everyone in the world.

4

BEARING COMPASSIONATE WITNESS
TO SUFFERING (PART 1)

THIS PRACTICE WILL HELP YOU:

▶ Increase awareness of and compassion for the suffering of others.

▶ Increase the ability to extend compassion regardless of the scope of suffering.

▶ Increase the ability to extend compassion in hopeless situations
and regardless of outcomes.

This practice and the following two are unlike most of the rest of the practices in this book in that you are invited to contemplate painful and difficult situations in the world. This can be very hard, but that difficulty is a crucial part of the efficacy of these practices, which have proved to be beneficial and effective for over a thousand years. But rest assured: after these three rather uncomfortable mental exercises, we'll be moving on to other practices, which are more lovely and beautiful to contemplate!

For this and all other emotionally painful exercises, please particularly concentrate during the "First Invite Love In" meditation at the beginning of your practice—it will sustain you.

STEP ONE: Use the "First Invite Love In" meditation on page 15 before you begin this guided meditation.

STEP TWO: Please follow the instructions below for the central part of this compassion practice.

STEP THREE: Use the "Seal with a Vow and Rejoice" meditation on page 22 when you conclude this guided meditation.

1. Imagine you have a child who has fallen into a swift river and is being carried away to certain death by drowning.

2. Visualize your child crying out to you to save him.

3. Imagine that you have no arms and there is no one around who can help.

4. See yourself running along the riverbank, unable to save your child.

5. Realize that there is absolutely nothing that you can do. There is no one who is going to arrive miraculously. There is no one you can run to. There is no way he can get out of this river.

There is no help in sight. There is nothing you can do to prevent your child—who is looking to you with fear and desperation—from drowning soon.

6. Understand that the only thing you can do is give him some emotional support so that he is not alone during this horrible situation. Meet his eyes and hold them with your own.

7. You can see that your child knows that he will soon drown and die; he knows you cannot save him.

8. You are looking at your child in order to give him the only thing you can at this point: your love and compassion, your witnessing, and your being there with him at this awful time.

9. Just imagine a child whom you have loved so deeply somehow slipping into a river that has an embankment so steep or is so swift that there is no possibility that he will get out by himself, and you have no arms and no way to use any other part of your body in order to save him. You are somewhere in the wilderness where there is no one around and no one who will come to save him. You are looking at him and you are seeing his fear and his desperation and his knowledge of his upcoming death. You are there with him, but unable to help. You are unable to prevent the end of his precious life.

10. Just hold that thought. Have your eyes look into the eyes of your child at this moment of his life.

Short Form

Imagine you have a child who fell into a swift river and is being carried away to certain death by drowning. Your child cries out to you to save him. Imagine that you have no arms and that you are running along the banks of the river, unable to save your child. There is no help in sight and nothing you can do to prevent your child, who is looking into your eyes with fear and desperation, from drowning soon.

5

Bearing Compassionate Witness
to Suffering (Part 2)

THIS PRACTICE WILL HELP YOU:

▶ Increase awareness of and compassion for the suffering of others.

▶ Increase the ability to extend compassion regardless of the scope of suffering.

▶ Increase the ability to extend compassion in hopeless
situations and regardless of outcomes.

This is the second one in the set of three that are a bit more difficult to contemplate, but we can get through them and they will serve to stretch your heart to feel compassion and peace. Remember, again, to focus with particular attention on the "First Invite Love In" meditation before you begin.

Step One: Use the "First Invite Love In" meditation on page 15 before you begin this guided meditation.

STEP TWO: Please follow the instructions below for the central part of this compassion practice.

STEP THREE: Use the "Seal with a Vow and Rejoice" meditation on page 22 when you conclude this guided meditation.

1. Think of a place in the world that is torn apart by war. Unfortunately, there are many such places in the world these days from which to choose. The place you select doesn't have to be a place where there has been a formal declaration of war, but could perhaps be a place where you know that people there are at war with each other.

2. Imagine yourself to be a mother in this place and that you've just discovered that your beloved child has suffered a very serious injury, one that is so severe that it will prevent your child from ever leading a normal life again. There is no way to fix this. There is no way to pray out of it. There is no way to get an operation. It is just an out-and-out loss that will mean a difficult life, suffering, and unhappiness for your child.

3. Imagine the specific sadness you would feel upon first seeing your injured child. Perhaps they are missing a limb, or they have lost their sight or some mental capacity, and so they never will walk or move freely again.

4. Now imagine how you would feel as a very loving mother whose beloved child will lead an impaired, painful, possibly unhappy life because of being caught in the crossfire of a war.

5. Take a moment to imagine mothers and fathers all across the world who face this kind of situation. Imagine yourself as one of them, and see the child and feel your sadness and compassion for them.

6. Now think about another country in the world where people are fighting and children can find themselves in harm's way. Imagine yourself as a mother in this country and, after a battle or a fight, coming upon your child who is hurt or wounded in such a way that they won't recover full health and ability.

7. Try this one more time in yet another country; unfortunately, there are more than three places in the world where these kinds of things are daily occurrences. Put yourself in the shoes of a mother in that country coming upon or being brought her injured child. Feel how the mother feels pain for the child, who will never fully recover. Feel how much love the mother has for the child, and how much sadness.

 ## SHORT FORM

Think of a place in the world that is war torn. Imagine your-self as a mother there finding out that one of her children has suffered a serious injury that will make it impossible for them to lead a normal life again. Imagine your sadness upon seeing your child with a missing limb, loss of sight, or loss of motion or mental ability. If possible, think about this in every place in the world where there is war now.

6

Bearing Compassionate Witness
to Suffering (Part 3)

THIS PRACTICE WILL HELP YOU:

▶ Increase awareness of and compassion for the suffering of others.

▶ Increase the ability to extend compassion regardless of the scope of suffering.

▶ Increase the ability to extend compassion in hopeless situations
and regardless of outcomes.

Don't forget to perform the "First Invite Love In" meditation with extra diligence before you perform this potentially difficult exercise.

STEP ONE: Use the "First Invite Love In" meditation on page 15 before you begin this guided meditation.

STEP TWO: Please follow the instructions below for the central part of this compassion practice.

STEP THREE: Use the "Seal with a Vow and Rejoice" meditation on page 22 when you conclude this guided meditation.

1. Think of someplace in the world where you know that people are starving to death. You can probably think of ten places in the world where people are starving at this very moment, but bring just one place into the forefront of your mind.

2. Imagine yourself as a mother in such a place, and in a circumstance where you are no longer able to provide food for your child.

3. Imagine that you hold a most beloved, beloved child in your arms who is in the last stages of starving to death.

4. Imagine that in this situation there is no miracle in sight. There is no possibility of being able to find food to save this child. There will be no medical rescue. The future is certain and the future is death for your beloved child.

5. Imagine yourself as this mother looking into the eyes of a child you love so much, and seeing the suffering of starving and the suffering of descending into death that you can do nothing whatsoever to relieve. Unfortunately, this is the case in many, many places. Mothers and fathers, brothers and sisters, uncles

and aunts are at this very moment with beloved ones who are starving to death before their eyes and they can do nothing to stop this painful, unfortunate, and seemingly unfair situation.

6. Imagine yourself now just for a moment as one of those mothers. You hold a child that you love with all of your heart, that you wish would be able to live and have a future, but who is dying because there is no food, who is starving to death and will soon die. You look, watch, and love this child. You see the suffering, and love this child.

7. Now think of yourself as a mother in every one of the places in the world where people are starving to death and where children are dying of hunger in the arms of their mothers. Imagine you are all those mothers holding all of those beloved children and all that you can offer is love; all you can do is to feel compassion and be there with them at this most awful and sad moment. Just contemplate that for a moment.

 Short Form

Imagine a place in the world where people are starving. Imagine yourself as a mother of a beloved child who is starving to death in your arms because you cannot find food to feed her. Imagine there is no possible hope of finding food before the child dies. Look into the child's eyes and see the suffering that you can do nothing to relieve. If possible, think about this in every place in the world where people are now starving to death.

7

Widening the Heart to Embrace the World with Loving-Kindness (Sunshine Metaphor)

THIS PRACTICE WILL HELP YOU:

▸ Increase feelings of loving-kindness to others.

▸ Create an association between a basic element of life (sunshine) and the wish for greater happiness for others.

▸ Expand the heart to embrace the greatest number of people possible and wish for their happiness.

STEP ONE: Use the "First Invite Love In" meditation on page 15 before you begin this guided meditation.

STEP TWO: Please follow the instructions below for the central part of this compassion practice.

STEP THREE: Use the "Seal with a Vow and Rejoice" meditation on page 22 when you conclude this guided meditation.

1. Imagine that when the sun shines brightly its rays of light are full of love and peace.

2. Imagine that this light with its feeling of love and peace is able to enter the minds and bodies of people.

3. Picture a beautiful sunny day and, in your mind, imbue the streaming sunlight with the qualities of love, peace, and happiness. Imagine that the sun has within it the capacity to transfer those feelings into the people that it touches, that it lights upon.

4. Now think about someone you love dearly and really care about.

5. See them in a beautiful field on a sunny day with the sun shining down on them with love and peace. See all the feelings of love and peace enter the person you picture.

6. See the person that you dearly love fill up with these feelings and become happier and happier as the sun touches them. See them feeling uplifted, relaxed, and expansive, and everything else one might feel if one were filled up with love and peace.

7. Now see every person in your family—your mother, your

father, your grandparents, your aunts, your uncles, your brothers and sisters—they are all in the field.

8. The sun is shining down on them with rays of light filled with love and peace.

9. See the love light entering them. See them all filling up with this.

10. Imagine them lighting up with this. Or imagine what their states of mind might be. Perhaps you might see how surprised and happy they would be to be experiencing this. Take a little while to see your whole family around you with the sun shining down on them and all this is happening.

11. Next add all your friends to the field. Put all your friends out there in the bright sun.

12. The rays of sunshine enter your friends' minds and bodies, and they feel loved. They feel peaceful. They feel strong. They feel hopeful.

13. Now we are going to stretch your capacity for compassion a bit further. Imagine that your whole neighborhood has come out. They are all outside their houses.

14. The sun is shining brightly. See your whole neighborhood, everybody around, perhaps five hundred or a thousand people, being filled with love and happiness. Imagine that. See that sun beaming down on them.

15. Now we are going to stretch our minds out to encompass the whole state. Imagine that everyone in the entire state comes out on this beautiful sunny day where the sunlight is filled with the intentionality and mindset of love and happiness.

16. The sunlight enters their minds and fills them up with strength, hope, and happiness. The whole state feels joyful and optimistic.

17. Then think that the whole country is having a beautiful, sunny, extraordinary day. Everyone steps outside to experience it.

18. See the sunlight come down and fill the whole country with hope, happiness, love, peace, and strength. Wouldn't that be wonderful?

19. Now, as the Earth turns, everyone all over the entire world has their day in the sun of happiness, love, and peace.

20. See the planet filled with a state of happiness, peace, and love. Contemplate that lovely thought.

 Short Form

Imagine that when the sun shines brightly its rays are full of love and peace, which enter the minds and bodies of someone you love dearly, filling them with happiness, peace, strength, and hope. Then imagine this happens to every person in your family when they stand in sunlight. Then to all of your friends. Then to everyone in your neighborhood, your state, your country, and ultimately to everyone in the world.

8

OVERCOMING ANGER AND BITTERNESS
WITH COMPASSION

THIS PRACTICE WILL HELP YOU:

▶ Increase awareness of and compassion for the suffering of others.

▶ Decrease the influence of anger and bitterness on your ability to be aware of and feel compassion for the suffering of others.

▶ Decrease feelings of alienation and divisiveness.

When practicing this exercise, it is important to be as objective as possible. You will be visualizing the unhappiness of a person you don't care for, and you should be careful *not to enjoy* doing so. Remove any thoughts of unpleasant interactions you have had with this person. Keep firmly in mind that there is no possible way that by thinking about this you could cause actual pain for this person, and that you are doing this exercise solely to create more empathy within yourself.

STEP ONE: Use the "First Invite Love In" meditation on page 15 before you begin this guided meditation.

STEP TWO: Please follow the instructions below for the central part of this compassion practice.

STEP THREE: Use the "Seal with a Vow and Rejoice" meditation on page 22 when you conclude this guided meditation.

1. Think about someone who annoys you or whom you really don't like. Bring this person into the forefront of your mind.

2. Think about something in their lives that is causing them to be unhappy. Try to think of the particulars of what might be wrong. If you don't know the person well enough to know what this might be, use your imagination to think about something that typically in the course of a person's life might cause them grief. Be careful not to take pleasure in their grief.

3. Take a moment to try to put yourself in this person's shoes at a time when something quite difficult has happened in their life, and they are upset about it. Just imagine that you are that person and something legitimately sad or difficult has happened to you. See and feel how upset they are about this situation.

4. Now step out of their shoes and be yourself again. Imagine that you have the ability to make right whatever it is that has gone wrong in their lives. You have this kind of magic ability.

5. Then imagine that you do that. You'll have to tailor this to the particular scenario that you thought of. Think that somehow you are able to undo whatever it is that happened or turn time back or give them what they needed that they didn't get. Whatever it is that would make them happy, imagine that you do that.

6. Take a minute to contemplate that sequence. See the person being upset. See yourself having whatever it takes to remedy the situation. You go to the person and you fix it. Imagine yourself making everything great again for the person. See yourself doing that.

7. Then imagine how peaceful and happy the person feels now that their life has improved. Something that was really bothering them has been resolved. Put yourself in their shoes again. The problem has been resolved, or it's disappeared, and things are good now. Feel how relieved they are. Feel how peaceful, happy, and relieved they are. Take a minute to contemplate that.

 ## Short Form

Think of someone who annoys you or whom you don't like. Think about something in their lives that is causing them to be unhappy. Imagine how sad and upset they are about this situation. Then imagine that you give them what they need to be happy or stop whatever is happening that is now making them unhappy. Imagine how peaceful and happy they feel now that their lives are better.

9

Widening the Heart to Embrace the World with Loving-Kindness (Snowfall Metaphor)

THIS PRACTICE WILL HELP YOU:

▸ Increase feelings of loving-kindness for others.

▸ Create an association with a basic element of life (precipitation) and the wish for greater happiness for others.

▸ Expand the heart to embrace the greatest number of people possible and wish for their happiness.

STEP ONE: Use the "First Invite Love In" meditation on page 15 before you begin this guided meditation.

STEP TWO: Please follow the instructions below for the central part of this compassion practice.

STEP THREE: Use the "Seal with a Vow and Rejoice" meditation on page 22 when you conclude this guided meditation.

1. Bring to mind a day when the snow is falling in light fluffy, fluffy flakes.

2. Imagine that every single snowflake is filled with a substance that brings complete and utter joy and happiness to living beings when it settles on them and dissolves into them.

3. Imagine a person that you love and care about standing out in a beautiful snowy day with these gorgeous fluffy snowflakes falling. Millions and millions of these are falling down around on the earth and tens of thousands land on your friend. They dissolve into your friend and fill your friend with inconceivable joy. Just see that. Your friend doesn't get soggy or wet or cold. These are miraculous snowflakes. These are spiritual snowflakes. The air is filled with these light, fluffy, joyful snowflakes.

4. Now see all of your friends walking out into the beautiful snowy day. Imagine as well every single member of your family—your aunts, your uncles, your parents, your grandparents, your cousins, your nieces, your nephews, your children, your brothers and sisters, and your grandchildren, or whatever relations you have—see them all out in this miraculous day. One by one, picture everyone you love standing outside in the glorious miraculous snowfall. No one is cold or wet. It is just beautiful.

5. This light fluffy snow is falling on each and every one of them and filling them up with pure happiness. Take a little while to see them fill up with this happiness as the snowflakes dissolve into them. It is beautiful.

6. Now, as usual, extend this visualization to encompass your entire neighborhood. Everyone in your neighborhood has recognized that it is a miraculous day. They step out into this beautiful snowfall with light fluffy snowflakes filled with inconceivable bliss that is dissolving into them.

7. See your entire neighborhood filling up with utter joy and happiness. What a sight!

8. Now imagine that word has spread and your entire state is aware that they are in a state of grace. They step out into the snowfall where light, fluffy, joyful snowflakes land on them and they fill up with inconceivable joy and happiness. Imagine that!

9. Next the entire country becomes aware of and is experiencing a shower of blessings, a snow shower of blessings. They all step out—children, grandparents, babies, everyone—to experience one snowflake after another, each one with the capacity to fill them with joy, happiness, and bliss, dissolving into them.

10. Then the entire world, everyone all over the world, is experiencing this blissful snowfall. Everyone steps out. The snow lands lightly and dissolves into every single human being on the planet. The entire planet of people is filled with bliss. Wouldn't that be a wonderful thing? Let's just contemplate for a moment that the entire world, every single human being, is experiencing utter joy and happiness.

⚝ Short Form

Imagine a day when snow is falling in light fluffy flakes. Imagine that each flake is filled with a substance that brings complete and utter joy and happiness to living beings. Imagine that endless snowflakes fall onto someone you love and dissolve into them, filling them with inconceivable joy and happiness. Then imagine this happens to all of your friends and every person in your family. Then to everyone in your neighborhood, your state, your country, and ultimately to everyone in the world.

10

Taking Compassion into Daily Life: Feeling Compassion for Strangers

THIS PRACTICE WILL HELP YOU:

▶ Increase awareness of and compassion for the suffering of others.

▶ Increase the aspiration to relieve the suffering of others.

▶ Take the practice of compassion into your daily life.

This guided meditation is a little different than the other compassion practices in that it is a set of instructions for something that you'll need to do out in the real world. So during this meditation, I'll help you to envision what you are going to do when you get out there. And remember—whenever practicing compassion for a stranger, it is important to do so discreetly so you do not make them uneasy.

STEP ONE: Use the "First Invite Love In" meditation on page 15 before you begin this guided meditation.

STEP TWO: Please follow the instructions below for the central part of this compassion practice.

STEP THREE: Use the "Seal with a Vow and Rejoice" meditation on page 22 when you conclude this guided meditation.

1. When you are out and about take a careful but discreet look at the face, posture, and demeanor of a perfect stranger.

2. Without staring too long and making this person uncomfortable, try to sense from their expression or how they move their body what might be making this person unhappy. Remember that you're not wishing unhappiness upon them; you are merely trying to identify what misfortune might have fallen into their life.

3. Once you have an idea, stop looking at the stranger but hold their image and possible pain in your mind.

4. Without looking at them, imagine that somehow you have the ability to change this person's life so that they can have whatever it is that they lack or resolve whatever issue is causing them sadness.

5. Imagine that you actually do it. Imagine that you are able to give the person what they need. See yourself in your mind doing this.

6. Then think about that person changing, and feeling very happy and peaceful.

7. Do that with as many strangers as you can.

 ## Short Form

Look carefully at a stranger. Try to imagine what makes this person unhappy in their life. Then imagine that you could change this person's life so that they have whatever they need to be happy. Think about this person feeling very happy and peaceful. Now try this with as many strangers as possible.

11

Increasing Generosity by Imagining Helping Others During a Famine

THIS PRACTICE WILL HELP YOU:

▸ Increase awareness of and compassion for the suffering of others.

▸ Increase the aspiration to relieve the suffering of others.

▸ Decrease attachment to possessions.

▸ Decrease selfishness.

▸ Increase generosity.

STEP ONE: Use the "First Invite Love In" meditation on page 15 before you begin this guided meditation.

STEP TWO: Please follow the instructions below for the central part of this compassion practice.

STEP THREE: Use the "Seal with a Vow and Rejoice" meditation on page 22 when you conclude this guided meditation.

1. Imagine that there has been a great famine and there is widespread terrible suffering and starvation. There is no food to be found anywhere, except in your home, where you miraculously have unending stores of highly nutritious food.

2. Imagine that you are at home and the doorbell rings. When you open it, you find at the door a stranger who is starving to death; they ask you for food. Just see that for a moment in your mind. The doorbell rings. There is someone there asking you for food and they are in desperate straits.

3. Imagine that your supply of food is limitless and that you have endless time and energy to help everyone in need.

4. Visualize yourself handing out lifesaving food to this person and see them weep with relief and gratitude.

5. Hear the doorbell ring again. Go to the door. See this poor person who is starving.

6. Give them this perfect, nutritious, wonderful food.

7. See them weep with relief and gratitude. Close the door.

8. The doorbell rings again. There's another person there who needs your help.

9. You give them this absolutely perfect food that they need.

10. See their relief and gratitude because of getting what they need to relieve their hunger and suffering. Feel your own strength and ability to continue to help, over and over, until no one is hungry.

11. Imagine yourself doing this again and again for as long as you can concentrate.

 ## Short Form

Imagine that there has been a great famine and there is widespread terrible suffering and starvation. There is no food to be found anywhere, but you have miraculously unending stores of highly nutritious food in your house. Imagine the doorbell rings and someone who is starving asks you for food. Visualize handing out lifesaving food to one visitor after another, each of whom weeps with relief and gratitude. Do this for as long as you can.

TAKING COMPASSION INTO DAILY LIFE: IMAGINING STRANGERS AS KIND MOTHERS

THIS PRACTICE WILL HELP YOU:

▸ Increase trust of others by creating a sense of kinship.

▸ Increase love for others by creating a sense of gratitude.

▸ Reduce feelings of divisiveness and "us vs. them."

▸ Take the feelings of greater trust, kinship, and gratitude toward others into the realm of daily life.

If you work with this practice enough over time you will be able to get to the point where you view all strangers with instantaneous love and gratitude. I have seen a person go through life like this. I have gone into drug stores, grocery stores, and shopping malls with a spiritual master who truly looked upon every person as having been his kindest mother in a past life. He greeted each person with an expression on his face that revealed he was feeling this way toward them. Of course, his experience of life was quite beautiful as a result. You can imagine the response of people who were greeted with such love. It caused everyone that he looked upon to beam with happiness. It was quite a lovely experience walking about with this person who seemed to actively practice this every moment of his day.

I think it takes quite awhile to get to the point where you can instantaneously and truly see a stranger this way, and feel that they have been a kind and loving mother, and feel that security with them and love and gratitude in response. But it is possible over time. And the results for the person who is practicing this and for the people who are greeted in such a fashion are tremendous—there is just happiness all around.

This is another one of the practices that you will do out in real life during the day ahead. And remember, whenever practicing compassion for strangers, to do so discreetly to avoid making them uncomfortable.

STEP ONE: Use the "First Invite Love In" meditation on page 15 before you begin this guided meditation.

STEP TWO: Please follow the instructions below for the central part of this compassion practice.

STEP THREE: Use the "Seal with a Vow and Rejoice" meditation on page 22 when you conclude this guided meditation.

1. You'll begin by looking at the face of a random stranger. Create a clear impression or picture of this person in your mind. Then turn away and hold that picture in your mind to continue with this visualization.

2. Imagine that, in a past life, this stranger had been the most loving and caring mother to you that you can conceive of. Even if you don't believe in past lives, use your imagination and picture this person as a mother who had taken care of your every need. They protected you from danger. They gave you everything that you needed to grow up feeling supported, comfortable, and loved. They made every sacrifice necessary in order to make sure that you had everything you needed and were happy throughout your childhood.

3. Imagine yourself as a child and see this person doing all of these loving, caring, protecting, shielding, developing, and nurturing things for you. Imagine what it would have been like to have a mother like that and that this person had been such a mother for you. Contemplate that for a moment.

4. Then think about how grateful you would have been to this person for having been such a kind mother. Imagine their love and support coming into you, and imagine your happiness and your gratitude to them in response.

5. Take some time to see yourself in different scenarios where this person, as your perfect mother, would be there to protect you and care for you and sustain you. See these scenes very specifically, and imagine yourself experiencing each one. In each scenario, feel yourself filling with love and gratitude to this person for having been such a kind mother.

6. Go through as many detailed scenarios as you want with this person in mind—of being taken care of by this person, of feeling supported and loved, and feeling in return tremendous love and gratitude toward them.

7. Then try this with another stranger.

8. Then try it again with another stranger.

9. Do this with as many strangers as possible.

 SHORT FORM

Look carefully at the face of a complete stranger. Imagine that in a past life this person had been the most loving and caring mother to you conceivable. Imagine that this person made every sacrifice possible to shield you from danger, comfort you in sadness, and attend to your every need. Then think about how grateful you would have been to this person when they were taking such kind care of you when you were a child. Now try this with as many strangers as possible.

13

CONNECTING THE BODY AND ACTIONS
WITH COMPASSION

THIS PRACTICE WILL HELP YOU:

▶ Increase feelings of loving-kindness toward others.

▶ Increase awareness of the role of your body and actions
as a means to express loving-kindness.

▶ Expand your heart to embrace and extend loving-kindness
to as many people as possible.

STEP ONE: Use the "First Invite Love In" meditation on page 15 before you begin this guided meditation.

STEP TWO: Please follow the instructions below for the central part of this compassion practice.

STEP THREE: Use the "Seal with a Vow and Rejoice" meditation on page 22 when you conclude this guided meditation.

1. Imagine that the spiritual being who supports you is filling you with endless pure love and peace. This is an inexhaustible supply that fills you from head to toe.

2. Now imagine that you are going to send that love and peace out in all directions in the form of rays of white light from the center of your head. This white light that radiates goodwill is constantly replenished by your spiritual supporter so you do not feel in any way drained by it.

3. First imagine that this white light that is imbued with feelings of love and peace extends a few inches around your head. Just see that until it is clear.

4. Now imagine yourself in the center of a map of your neighborhood. You are in the very center of your neighborhood and you are radiating this white light that is extending out from the center of your head, a light that has endless feelings of love and peace within it.

5. Imagine that the light extends out so that it fills your neighborhood. This wonderful white light can go through walls, buildings, and underground. It touches everyone in your neighborhood.

6. When the light touches them, it causes them to act and think and interact with others from a place of love and peace. It causes all their actions to be peaceful and loving.

7. See what that would be like for your whole neighborhood if everyone were moving, were using their bodies, out of pure kindness and peacefulness.

8. You can try this with one person after another to get used to the idea. See one person after another filling with a feeling of peace and love, and then moving in a way motivated by that feeling.

9. Then imagine this happening to everyone on your whole street, and then your entire neighborhood.

10. Next imagine you are standing in the center of a mental map of your entire state.

11. See the never-ending, constantly replenished source of white light that is emanating from the center of your head reaching out and lighting upon everybody in your entire state.

12. Now they all move with peace and love; they all act from a place of peace and love. Take some time to imagine that.

13. Next see yourself in the center of a mental map or image of your entire country. See white light extending out, reaching out, to everyone from a place in the center of your head.

14. Love and peace moves out along those rays. They light upon and touch every single person in your country.

15. The entire country fills with white light and moves from a place of peace and love.

16. Then your mental map stretches further. It stretches into the entire world. See the white light at the center of your head extend out to the entire world. Every single person on the planet is touched by it.

17. See them fill with this light and feel profound feelings of love and peacefulness.

18. Then see them all move, act, and use their bodies with peace, love, and kindness.

19. Just imagine the white light coming from a never-ending source of peace and love in you and extending out across the entire planet as it is envisioned in your mental map.

20. It reaches out to the whole world, every single person.

21. It enters them and animates them to move from a place of peace, kindness, love, and compassion. Hold that thought for as long as you can.

 ## Short Form

Imagine a white light in the center of your head that sends out rays of love and peace in all directions. Imagine the white light extends a few inches around your body. Continue extending the light until it encompasses your neighborhood, then your whole state, then your country, and finally until it bathes the entire earth in white rays and everyone on earth acts out of love and peace.

14

INCREASING GENEROSITY BY IMAGINING GIVING ALL TO SAVE THE LIFE OF A LOVED ONE

THIS PRACTICE WILL HELP YOU:

▸ Increase awareness of and compassion for the suffering of others.

▸ Increase the aspiration to relieve the suffering of others.

▸ Decrease attachment to possessions.

▸ Decrease selfishness.

▸ Increase generosity.

STEP ONE: Use the "First Invite Love In" meditation on page 15 before you begin this guided meditation.

STEP TWO: Please follow the instructions below for the central part of this compassion practice.

STEP THREE: Use the "Seal with a Vow and Rejoice" meditation on page 22 when you conclude this guided meditation.

1. Bring to the forefront of your mind someone you love dearly. This could be a real person or, if necessary, it could be an imaginary person of the type whom you feel you could love dearly.

2. Imagine that this person who is precious to you could die if they do not receive a lifesaving operation very soon. They have a terminal illness or some other medically critical situation that requires a very expensive operation that must happen immediately, or they will die.

3. Now understand that they don't have the money to pay for the operation. They don't have health insurance and the state isn't going to come to the aid of this person. They have no family or friends who could help. There is no one else they can turn to for this. The only person who can possibly help them is you.

4. Next imagine that you don't have enough money in your bank account to help them and you don't have any place to go to for a loan. All you can do at this point is sell everything that you have. If you have a home, you will have to mortgage it. In order to help this person live you will have to sell every last possession that you have. You are going to be all right after this situation. You have a source of income and you will be able to rebuild your financial security after this. You are not putting yourself at risk. But you are going to have to go to the bank,

clear out your bank account, and sell your home, if you own one, and everything that you have in order to come up with the money quickly that this person—your dearly beloved friend or family member—needs in order to live. Take a minute to visualize this situation.

5. I will lead you through this scenario again. Imagine that someone you dearly love is in a situation where their entire normal support system is gone. They are in a critical situation medically, and they come to you saying, "Can you help me?" First see that in your mind.

6. Then see yourself going to your bank and clearing out your bank account. If you own a house or cars or other things of great value, see yourself selling all of them. If you have any stocks, bonds, or the like, imagine yourself cashing them out. You are selling your jewelry. You are selling everything.

7. Then see yourself giving this person the money and visualize how happy and relieved they are that you have come to their rescue and that they will now be assured of a healthy future.

8. Let's go through this again. Your friend or beloved family member's life is in danger. They require a medical operation that is extremely costly. They come to you for help.

9. See yourself going to your bank. Clearing out your bank account. Putting your house or car up for sale. Selling everything that you own so that your beloved friend or family member will be able to live and be healthy.

10. See how happy and relieved they are.

 ## SHORT FORM

Imagine that someone you love very dearly will die if they do not receive a lifesaving operation very soon. They don't have the money to pay for the operation and neither do you. The only way you can save this loved one's life is to clear out your bank account and sell all of your assets to pay for the operation. Visualize going to the bank to get the money, doing whatever is necessary to sell all of your assets, and giving the money to the person. Visualize the person's relief and happiness to know they will have the funds to pay for their lifesaving operation.

15

Opening the Heart by Loosening the Grip of Possessiveness

THIS PRACTICE WILL HELP YOU:

▶ Increase awareness of and compassion for the suffering of others.

▶ Increase the aspiration to relieve the suffering of others.

▶ Decrease attachment to possessions.

▶ Decrease selfishness.

▶ Increase generosity.

STEP ONE: Use the "First Invite Love In" meditation on page 15 before you begin this guided meditation.

STEP TWO: Please follow the instructions below for the central part of this compassion practice.

STEP THREE: Use the "Seal with a Vow and Rejoice" meditation on page 22 when you conclude this guided meditation.

1. Think about the five things that you own that are your most favorite, prized possessions. These are the five things that if your house were burning down you would run to gather together to save. These are the things that you are the most proud of owning, or the things that you feel the best about yourself when you are wearing or using. They are the five things that people identify with you and that you feel express or represent who you are best. Choose the five things that you would be most upset about losing.

2. Now bring to mind the five people that you love and respect most. See them. Next imagine that they are ill, that they are dying.

3. Now think that your five objects are imbued with a magical substance that is a perfect chemical match for what those five people need in order to live. There is some kind of plague or chemical imbalance that they have for which your five objects are the perfect remedy.

4. So see the five people. Think that they are in a life-threatening situation requiring something that your five objects have imbued within them. Imagine that the only way these people can be saved is to have the object with them at all times, otherwise they will die. They need your possession.

5. Now you will see yourself taking each object in turn and giving it away permanently and irreversibly to one of the five people. You will see with each person how relieved and grateful they are as they walk away with the object that you have so generously given them to save their life.

6. Let's start with object number one. See person number one come up to you. See yourself hand the object to them.

7. See how relieved, happy, and grateful they are. They walk away with it, and you'll never see it again. But they will live a healthy life now.

8. Let's take object number two. Person number two comes up to you. You give it to them.

9. See how relieved and happy they are now knowing that they are going to be able to live a normal life and be healthy. They walk away with it. You let it go forever.

10. Take object number three. Person number three comes up. They have a terrible plague. Your object is imbued with whatever it is that will relieve them of the problem, but now they will have it with them all the time. They take it from you.

11. They are so grateful, so relieved, and so joyful. See them walk away with it forever.

12. Take object number four. Person number four arrives in dire straits and is going to die. You give them the object that is imbued with a magical quality that will save their life.

13. They are so relieved and happy. They are so grateful to you, and they walk with it forever.

14. See object number five and person number five in terrible need and very frightened. You give the object that will save their life.

15. They are so grateful. They are so happy. They are so relieved. They are joyful. They are going to live! They walk away with the object forever.

16. Now we are going to step this visualization up a bit. Imagine that there is a plague in the area and there are hundreds of people stricken with it.

17. Imagine that everything that you own in your home is imbued with what they need to save their lives.

18. There is a line of people coming up to your doorstep.

19. One by one, you hand them every object that you own. One by one, see how happy and relieved they are that you have given them what they need to save their lives.

20. You can continue to work on that visualization on your own for as long as you can.

 ## Short Form

Think of the five favorite objects you own. Next imagine each object has a substance that will save the life of the five people in your life whom you care most deeply about. For some reason, each person will definitely die if you do not give them one of your prized possessions. Now imagine that you give away permanently and irreversibly the object to the person. Next visualize how relieved and grateful they are as they walk away with the object. Then if you can, imagine that there are hundreds of people whose lives are in danger and that one by one you give away everything you own in order to save their lives.

16

Widening the Heart to Embrace the World with Loving-Kindness (Song Metaphor)

THIS PRACTICE WILL HELP YOU:

▸ Increase feelings of loving-kindness toward others.

▸ Create an association with the sound of your voice and the wish for greater happiness for others.

▸ Expand the heart to embrace the greatest number of people possible and wish for their happiness.

STEP ONE: Use the "First Invite Love In" meditation on page 15 before you begin this guided meditation.

STEP TWO: Please follow the instructions below for the central part of this compassion practice.

STEP THREE: Use the "Seal with a Vow and Rejoice" meditation on page 22 when you conclude this guided meditation.

1. Imagine that you can sing a song that is so exquisite and so imbued with love, peace, and happiness that it fills those who hear it with indescribable happiness. Even if you are not usually a very good singer, somehow this song can come pouring out of you and transform the minds of those around you into a place of pure bliss.

2. Now imagine that hearing it will cause them to sing the same melody in the same way with the same quality. So imagine that when this beautiful melody pours out from you—an absolutely exquisite song—another person will hear it and will be immediately able and willing to sing the same song in the same way with the same quality that will bring amazing happiness, great bliss, and peacefulness to other people who hear it.

3. So first just imagine this song—this heavenly, transcendent, gloriously beautiful music that clears the mind. Imagine that melody and that quality welling up in you; you open your mouth and it pours forth miraculously. Take a few seconds to try that out.

4. Next bring to mind everyone that you care deeply about. Perhaps that is two people, or ten, or fifty. However many people that might be, take a moment now and see yourself in a lovely place near them. They can see you. They can hear you.

5. And then see yourself singing this exquisite song.

6. Then see them all feeling tremendous happiness and peace because of hearing it.

7. Then see that they in turn start to sing the song themselves with the same quality of infectious joy. Just picture that for a moment.

8. Next add to this picture in your mind another circle of people whom you don't like. These are people you know and for some reason you don't like them.

9. Imagine that they can hear you singing this beautiful song.

10. The song conveys a great state of happiness and it fills them with happiness. See the people you don't like filling up with indescribable happiness.

11. And then see the song welling up in them and see them singing it exquisitely. So you've got people you like and people that you don't like hearing the song, and everyone experiences indescribable happiness and then wells up with the song of happiness and sings it.

12. Now imagine you're in a sports stadium on a glorious day and you've got the people you care about and the people you don't like, and a stadium full of strangers.

13. The song wells up in you. This exquisite indescribably happy song comes out.

14. Everybody in the whole stadium experiences indescribable happiness.

15. From the core of their being the same song wells up and they all begin to sing it. Take a minute to envision that the glorious idea.

16. Now see a vast landscape where in all directions as far as you can see there are people everywhere. You are in the center of that.

17. You sing a song that has in it exquisite, glorious, indescribable happiness. It is a beautiful thing. You sing it perfectly.

18. The feeling of bliss and joy infuses everybody as far as you can see. They all hear it and feel indescribable happiness.

19. The same song wells up in them. They sing it and it affects everyone within earshot of them.

20. Take a little time to first see a vast sea of people in all directions and then see yourself singing the melody and reaching people's minds, and that in this vast sea of people everyone's mind becomes filled with indescribable happiness and bliss, and they all begin singing in the same way.

 ## Short Form

Imagine that you can sing a song that is so exquisite that it brings indescribable happiness to everyone who hears it. Imagine that when someone hears this song they, too, start singing in the same way. First sing the song to everyone you care deeply about, then to people you don't like, then to a stadium full of strangers, then to a vast expanse of people as far as the eye can see. Remember to imagine hearing everyone singing the song after you first sing it to them.

17

THINKING OF PEOPLE YOU DON'T LIKE
AS KIND MOTHERS

THIS PRACTICE WILL HELP YOU:

▶ Increase trust of others by creating a sense of kinship.

▶ Increase love for others by creating a sense of gratitude.

▶ Reduce feelings of divisiveness and "us vs. them."

▶ Reduce or overcome feelings of anger and bitterness
toward individuals or groups.

We're almost halfway through the forty practices and perhaps ready to begin building upon our foundation of practice. In the first round we began by thinking of someone whom we care about as having been our mother in a past life. In the second round we thought of a stranger that way. And now we're going to work on opening our hearts even further by using this same process and thinking about someone we don't like as having been our mother in a past life. This will certainly be a challenge, but it is a challenge that can greatly expand our hearts.

STEP ONE: Use the "First Invite Love In" meditation on page 15 before you begin this guided meditation.

STEP TWO: Please follow the instructions below for the central part of this compassion practice.

STEP THREE: Use the "Seal with a Vow and Rejoice" meditation on page 22 when you conclude this guided meditation.

1. Start by thinking about someone who has upset, irritated, or angered you in some fashion. Choose someone that you know who has made you angry or disturbed your mind. As a result, you don't like them very much. Think of that person. Put them clearly in the forefront of your mind.

2. Try to put the circumstances that caused you to dislike this person, or to feel hurt or upset, out of your mind. If you can, let that just drop. Let it recede from your mind. Do whatever you can do to calm that negative reaction and association down.

3. We're going to imagine that this person in a past life was the kindest, most caring, loving, protective, and supportive mother to you possible. Even if you don't believe in past lives, use your imagination.

4. You are going to consider the core essence, the pure soul that is at the center of this person—consider that part, not your

relationship with them now. If you have trouble imagining how this person, who is so irritating to you now, could ever have been your kind mother, imagine that something has gone askew for them in this life. Whatever trouble has happened to them in their current life has no bearing on your past relationship. Consider only that core essence of the person.

5. Then put yourself in the scenario of a past life where this person was an incredibly loving mother for you.

6. Take some time to envision this past life with this person—the essence of them—in the visage and the embodiment of an extraordinarily sensitive, kind, caring, and protective mother. Think about some typical scenes in the life of the child with a loving mother where this person took care of you.

7. Imagine that you are a baby and you cry. This person—in a past life who has at their essence the same person you don't like now—runs to you, looks concerned, picks you up, and discovers what was wrong. And she makes it all just fine. You're happy. You feel so loved.

8. Or imagine that you are older. You are a toddler. A dog barks or there is a loud noise. You're startled and you're frightened. This person as your kind and loving mother picks you up and

makes you feel secure. She gives you a hug and smiles at you so that you can see that everything is just fine and there's nothing to worry about. She's right there when something frightens you, ready take to care of you.

9. Or imagine you've been out playing. You've been running hard. You are hot and sweaty. You are incredibly thirsty. Your kind mother—who in your current life you don't like—sees that and tells you to stop for a second. She gives you something to drink so that you won't get dehydrated. She is looking out for you.

10. Now choose a few scenarios that represent for you what an incredibly kind mother would do. Take a little time to run through those for yourself. Imagine this person doing these things for you as your mother. Then imagine how grateful you would be to this wonderfully kind mother. So as the mother does something to take care of you and is loving, protective, and nurturing, imagine that you are so loving and grateful for their kindness in return. And it's this person that you don't like, or the essence of this person in a past life, who is this wonderful mother for you.

11. It would be good to continue with this practice thinking of other people who have annoyed, angered, irritated, or

infuriated you and go through the whole exercise again with
each of these people.

 ## Short Form

Think about someone who has upset, irritated, or angered you.
Imagine that in a past life this person had been the most loving
and caring mother to you conceivable. Imagine that this person
made every sacrifice possible to shield you from danger, comfort you in sadness, and attend to your every need. Then think
about how grateful you would have been to this person when
they were taking such kind care of you when you were a child.
Now try this with as many people as possible who have upset,
hurt, or angered you in the past.

18

Increasing Loving-Kindness by Rejoicing for the Good Fortune of Others (Happiness Version)

THIS PRACTICE WILL HELP YOU:

▸ Increase loving-kindness toward others.

▸ Reduce feelings of envy or jealousy.

▸ Increase the ability to rejoice for others.

▸ Overcome the view of life as a zero-sum game.

In this exercise we will be working on controlling and eliminating feelings of envy and jealousy. What we're going to do is think of a series of miraculously great things happening for another person and rejoice in the fact that things are going so well for them. Before we get into this I think it is helpful to look at the situation rationally and acknowledge that when good things happen for another person that generally does not mean that bad things will happen for you. Life is not a zero-sum game. So what we're going to try to do is to see wonderful things happening for another person and not feel diminished or think that this in any way means there will be less happiness for you. That person is just having a great time; they didn't take anything away from you. We can just be happy for them. If it helps, you can imagine as a starting point that equally wonderful things have happened for you and that nothing can take away your standing in the world and your access to your sources of happiness.

STEP ONE: Use the "First Invite Love In" meditation on page 15 before you begin this guided meditation.

STEP TWO: Please follow the instructions below for the central part of this compassion practice.

STEP THREE: Use the "Seal with a Vow and Rejoice" meditation on page 22 when you conclude this guided meditation.

1. Bring to mind someone that you like a great deal, someone for whom you should wish every happiness. This could be somebody in your family. It could be a friend or your spouse. It could be someone you don't know personally, but really like a great deal. Whoever it is, bring that person clearly into your mind.

2. Then imagine that they now have tremendous good health. They are brimming with terrific health and strength physically. You can see they are relaxed, strong, and fit. They feel great.

3. And then imagine that things happen in their work such that they meet with success at every turn. As a result, they get more money. A tremendous amount of money is now rolling in for them. They are truly wealthy.

4. Now imagine that they are also receiving fame and recognition for what they've done and are getting a lot of praise from the people around them. They're getting an award or they are in the newspaper. Articles are being written about them.

5. Take a little time and play that scenario in your mind; you see all these terrific things happening for that person and you completely rejoice for them without feeling that their success in any way diminishes you in the eyes of the world or in your own eyes. You realize that their happiness does not take anything away from your own ability to do well in the world and be happy. See it all unfolding where the person is succeeding in everything and you are happy and have eliminated even the tiniest trace of envy and jealousy. Take some time to think about that.

6. Now we are going to do something a little harder. Bring to mind someone who has done something mean or unkind to you in the past.

7. Now imagine that wonderful things are happening to this person—just like you imagined them happening for the person that you really like. And again, it's not taking anything away from you. Imagine their career takes off and they acquire wealth and fame. They gain power. But they don't use it in any way against you. They're not even thinking about you. It doesn't affect your relationship. It doesn't affect your standing in the world.

8. See yourself fully rejoicing for them and being happy for their good fortune. Feel yourself free of jealousy. Be free of bitterness.

Short Form

Think of someone you like a lot and imagine that their life takes a miraculous turn for the good and they are blessed with great health, wealth, and success of every kind. Imagine yourself being happy for them without any trace of jealousy, bitterness, or envy. Next think of someone who at some point in your life did something mean or unkind to you that had really upset you. Now imagine that their lives take a miraculous turn for the good and they too are blessed with great health, wealth, and success of every kind. Imagine yourself being happy for them without any trace of jealousy, bitterness, or envy.

Reducing Pride and Egotism through Remorse

THIS PRACTICE WILL HELP YOU:

▸ Reduce feelings of pride and egotism.

▸ Increase ability to feel remorse for acts that caused suffering
of any kind to others.

▸ Increase awareness of and compassion for the suffering of others.

STEP ONE: Use the "First Invite Love In" meditation on page 15 before
you begin this guided meditation.

STEP TWO: Please follow the instructions below for the central part of
this compassion practice.

STEP THREE: Use the "Seal with a Vow and Rejoice" meditation on page
22 when you conclude this guided meditation.

1. Think of someone to whom you've been unkind or unfair at some point in your life. Think back over your life and find a time when for whatever reason you did not give someone a reasonable, kind response to something that they did or something that they didn't do. Someone to whom you know in your heart of hearts that you were unfair or mean. This happens in everyone's life. We're not perfect all the time. There are circumstances that sometimes bring the worst out in us. Think of one of those kinds of times and that person.

2. Now imagine going to the person and apologizing profusely and sincerely for what you did. See yourself visiting this person or calling the person up.

3. See yourself expressing remorse for what you did and regret for any hurt, inconvenience, damage, or bad feelings that you might have caused them. Imagine yourself being very sincere as you do this—giving no excuses for yourself, no explanations, no rationales, and no way out of taking responsibility for what you did and for what happened to them as a result. You made a mistake. You are sorry that you hurt their feelings or upset them and you really truly wish that you could take it back— that it had never happened and that they were never hurt.

4. Now imagine that this act of contrition on your part completely heals the hurt or angry feelings that they may have been

harboring in their minds. Imagine that apologizing and being sincerely remorseful takes away any bad feelings, bitterness, sadness, or pain that they may have had. It just takes that completely out of their minds. It heals them. Let's take a little time to think that through and make sure that you really see the person feeling so much better as a result of your sincere apology.

5. Good. Now imagine everyone in the world going to people that they have hurt or been unkind or unfair to and making sincere apologies.

6. Imagine that this heals the wounds of the people who are receiving the sincere apologies.

7. Take some time with this. Really imagine people all over the world feeling remorseful about hurtful acts, going to express their apologies, and thus healing the wounded parties so that no pain remains anywhere in the world.

Think of someone to whom you have been unkind or unfair at some point in your life. Imagine going to the person and apologizing profusely and sincerely for what you did and that this act of contrition completely heals the hurt or angry feelings they have harbored in their minds. Imagine everyone in the world going to people whom they have hurt or been unkind or unfair to and doing the same thing with the same healing results.

Increasing Loving-Kindness by Rejoicing for the Good Fortune of Others (Wealth Version)

THIS PRACTICE WILL HELP YOU:

- ▸ Increase loving-kindness toward others.

- ▸ Increase ability to rejoice for others.

- ▸ Decrease envy and jealousy.

- ▸ Overcome or reduce egotism and the implicit view of life as a zero-sum game.

In this practice we are going to be working on stretching your heart such that you can truly rejoice in the good fortune of other people without any reserve or self-concern. We will be imagining other people suddenly coming into great wealth and we're going to practice being happy and rejoicing for them without any accompanying worry for ourselves. We want to be particularly on the lookout for any feelings of jealousy, possessiveness, etc.

Remember that in this scenario the great good fortune of other people and their sudden wealth has nothing to do with you. It doesn't mean that you won't also acquire great wealth later yourself or have any less wealth than you do now. It's simply a good thing for them and completely neutral in terms of its impact on you—except insofar as you rejoice for them.

STEP ONE: Use the "First Invite Love In" meditation on page 15 before you begin this guided meditation.

STEP TWO: Please follow the instructions below for the central part of this compassion practice.

STEP THREE: Use the "Seal with a Vow and Rejoice" meditation on page 22 when you conclude this guided meditation.

1. Think of somebody you like. Imagine they've won the lottery or they came into a great inheritance. For some reason they have an enormous amount of money suddenly. Remember that this in no way affects you or your relationship with them. Nothing has changed for you; your friend has simply had good fortune.

2. See how great their life is now.

3. Take pleasure in your mind for them. Feel their happiness and rejoice for them. Take a moment to see that.

4. Let's think of another person that you like. It may not be someone you know personally, but they are someone for whom you'd be happy if suddenly they came into a great deal of wealth.

5. See how happy they are because of their good fortune.

6. Rejoice and celebrate for them.

7. Next try thinking this way of your whole family. Imagine every single one of them suddenly became very wealthy. They are all going to have happy, comfortable lives and always be taken care of financially.

8. See them all incredibly happy.

9. See yourself feeling great happiness for them. Remember that their good luck does not adversely affect you. Nothing has changed except that no one in your family will ever have to worry about money again.

10. Okay. Let's take it a bit further. Think of everybody that you know. Somehow a check has arrived in everyone's mail. There is a surprise in their bank account, or there's a strange event where everybody buys a lottery ticket and they all win. They are all very wealthy. They are all going to be well off now for the rest of their lives.

11. This is a time of great happiness for everyone. Rejoice for them.

12. Now let's stretch your heart a little further. Imagine that your entire neighborhood becomes wealthy. Perhaps there's some great philanthropist who gives everyone in the whole area wealth. Who knows what the rationale is? It could be that there is a great sociology experiment where they decided to see what would happen if they gave an entire neighborhood financial wherewithal for the rest of their lives. Hooray! Now everybody is doing very, very well. They are all wealthy. See everybody feeling comfortable and happy that their financial security is assured.

13. Feel their happiness. Feel happy for them. Rejoice.

14. Let's stretch this visualization out to cover your entire state. Imagine that everybody in the whole state becomes comfortable financially. They've all come into sudden tremendous wealth.

15. See their relief and their happiness at this. See their sense of security and rejoice at their good fortune.

16. Open your heart even further. Extend it now to include the entire country. Imagine that everybody in the entire country is very, very wealthy. And they are very, very happy about it.

17. Open your heart and feel very happy that the entire country has good fortune. Everything is going to be fine financially for the rest of their lives.

18. Now see the entire planet showered with financial blessings. Everyone has a great deal of money. Everyone has everything that they need to do everything that they want. Everyone is celebrating.

19. See this planet of happiness, this planet of the financial security and abundance, and rejoice.

 SHORT FORM

Imagine that everyone you know suddenly comes into great wealth. Think of this person by person with joy for their good fortune and without any trace of jealousy, bitterness, or envy. Now imagine that great wealth comes to everyone in your neighborhood, your state, your country, and ultimately to everyone in the world.

21

Taking Compassion into Daily Life: Speaking to Strangers with Loving-Kindness

THIS PRACTICE WILL HELP YOU:

▶ Increase loving-kindness toward others.

▶ Create an association with the sound of your voice
and the expression of loving-kindness.

▶ Take the practice of loving-kindness into your daily life.

This is one of the practices that is to be used in real life as you go about your day. In this mental exercise you are going to imagine that your voice and words carry within them the power and the intentionality of love and compassion.

STEP ONE: Use the "First Invite Love In" meditation on page 15 before you begin this guided meditation.

STEP Two: Please follow the instructions below for the central part of this compassion practice.

STEP THREE: Use the "Seal with a Vow and Rejoice " meditation on page 22 when you conclude this guided meditation.

1. When you are about to speak to someone, first connect with a feeling of love within yourself. This is a non-specific love. You don't have to find something lovable about the people with whom you are about to speak. Think that love simply wells up within you and fills you.

2. Next imagine that the love that you feel is conveyed to others simply through the sound of your voice; you speak to someone and they feel loved as a result. This love is not dependent on the content of what you say—for example, you might just be about to thank the clerk at your grocery store for bagging your groceries.

3. Then form the intention of giving the person a feeling of being loved.

4. Then when you speak, imagine the feeling of love extending along the sound waves of your voice to enter the mind of the person you are speaking to. Imagine that at some level they feel loved as a result.

5. Envision that your words and the sound of your voice have a peaceful, soothing, and beneficial effect on the person who hears them.

6. Do this as much as possible today and every day.

 ## SHORT FORM

Imagine that your voice and words carry the power of love in them. Before you talk to someone, have the intention in your mind that, no matter what it is that you say, somehow your words will have a peaceful, soothing, and beneficial effect on the person. Try this with a stranger, perhaps at a checkout counter at a store. Do this as much as possible.

Imagining Others Are Cleansed
of the Source of Suffering

THIS PRACTICE WILL HELP YOU:

▸ Increase awareness of and compassion for the suffering of others.

▸ Increase the aspiration to relieve others of suffering by eliminating
the source of suffering within their own minds.

▸ Expand your heart and mind to embrace as many
people as possible.

In this practice we're going to be envisioning the spiritual and emotional cleansing of another person. Before we begin I want to remind
you that in this compassion practice—as with all others in this book—
we are engaged in training our own minds to feel compassion and
loving-kindness; this is not a prayer or an attempt to actually alter or
influence the state of mind or emotional or physical health of another

person in real life. Hopefully, this may lead to a greater inclination to take such steps in real life to help others, but this itself is not in any way an alternate means to provide actual relief for the mental suffering of others.

STEP ONE: Use the "First Invite Love In" meditation on page 15 before you begin this guided meditation.

STEP TWO: Please follow the instructions below for the central part of this compassion practice.

STEP THREE: Use the "Seal with a Vow and Rejoice" meditation on page 22 when you conclude this guided meditation.

1. Begin by bringing to mind someone you care deeply about. Think of someone for whom you would wish every happiness and peace of mind.

2. Imagine that the person is surrounded by a field of white light that has the miraculous power to cleanse negativity in all forms—physical, emotional, or spiritual—in their mind and body.

3. Now imagine that all the pores in the person's body open to let in or to draw in this cleansing white light.

4. Visualize a force or an intentionality of the white light that causes it to go into the person's body through the open pores and then enter their mind.

5. Imagine that the white light washes away the residual mental effects of everything negative that has ever been done to the person and anything negative that the person may have done to others.

6. Visualize this cleansing white light filling the person, washing away all of those negative effects on their state of mind. All of the negativity in their minds—whether a result of their actions or the actions of others—gets washed away by this white cleansing light coming into them.

7. Imagine that the negativity leaves them through their lower orifices or the bottoms of their feet as a harmless soot or gray mist.

8. Imagine that as a result the person feels peaceful and experiences a sense of clarity and a greater capacity for love and joy.

9. Finish by envisioning that the person's pores close up again to seal in and protect their new purity of mind.

10. Next bring to mind all of your friends and every person in your family. See them as group in front of you and imagine that all the pores in their bodies open up.

11. See them being surrounded by this white light that has the miraculous quality of being able to cleanse mental negativity and see it entering their bodies through their open pores.

12. Think that all of the negativity in their minds that's been created as a result of their own negative actions or because of negative things that have happened to them drops away and out of them through their lower orifices.

13. Imagine this leaves them with a state of mind filled with peace, clarity, love, joy, and bliss and that the pores in their bodies close again to seal in and protect their new state of mind.

14. Now imagine that a cleansing white light surrounds everyone in the neighborhood and that it enters their bodies through their open pores.

15. See their mental negativity dropping away, leaving them with a sense of peace, clarity, love, and bliss.

16. Next see your entire state surrounded by this extraordinary miraculous white cleansing light.

17. Imagine that the pores in the bodies of everyone in your state open up and that the white light enters them and takes away all traces of negativity in their minds.

18. Imagine that the negativity drops away out of them like soot or gray mist and that as a result their mind has greater clarity and they experience feelings of peacefulness, bliss, joy, and love.

19. See the pores on their bodies close, sealing in and protecting their lovely new state of mind.

20. Now open your heart and mind to expand this visualization to include your entire country. Envision a glorious cloud of miraculous healing white light descending on the country.

21. See everyone's pores open up and the white light entering them. See all the negative thoughts, feelings, and physical effects as a result of having experienced negativity or acted, thought, or spoken in a negative fashion to other people—see all of that being washed away by the white cleansing light. It goes out through their feet and lower orifices like gray mist or soot.

22. Imagine that as a result everyone has gained a beautiful state of mind of peacefulness, clarity, bliss, joy, and love that is sealed in as their pores close up.

23. Lastly, visualize that the entire planet is enveloped in this cleansing, healing white light.

24. Think that everyone on the planet has his or her pores open up to receive the blessing of the white light that comes into them and washes away all negativity, all effects of negative things happening to them or negative things that they have done.

25. See the negativity washing down out of them like soot or gray mist, leaving them with a state of peacefulness, happiness, love, joy, bliss, and clarity.

26. End by visualizing that the pores on everyone's bodies all over the planet close up, sealing in and protecting this blissful new state of mind.

Think of someone you care deeply about and imagine that the person is surrounded by a field of white light that has the miraculous power to cleanse negativity in all forms. Imagine that all the pores in this person's body open up and that the cleansing white light enters their body, washing away all the mental effects of everything negative that has been done to them or that they have done to others. The negativity comes out of their pores and their lower orifices as soot or gray mist leaving this person with a mental state of peace, clarity, love, and joy. The pores then close to seal in and protect the purity of this person's state of mind. Next imagine this sequence happening to all of your friends and every person in your family. Then to everyone in your neighborhood, your state, your country, and ultimately to everyone in the world.

23

Taking the Practice of Compassion into Daily Life: Looking at Strangers with Loving-Kindness

THIS PRACTICE WILL HELP YOU:

▸ Increase loving-kindness toward others.

▸ Increase trust of others by creating a sense of kinship.

▸ Increase love for others by creating a sense of gratitude.

▸ Reduce feelings of divisiveness and "us vs. them."

▸ Create the association that your eyes can convey loving-kindness.

▸ Take the practice of loving-kindness into daily life.

This is a practice that you will be using throughout the day ahead in the real world. What you will be doing is looking strangers in the eye and smiling warmly at them while at the same time imagining that they have been a kind mother to you in an imaginary past life.

STEP ONE: Use the "First Invite Love In" meditation on page 15 before you begin this guided meditation.

STEP TWO: Please follow the instructions below for the central part of this compassion practice.

STEP THREE: Use the "Seal with a Vow and Rejoice" meditation on page 22 when you conclude this guided meditation.

1. Choose a random stranger.

2. Try to think that they were your mother in an envisioned past life.

3. Look them in the eye and give them a quick warm smile with the intention of giving them a little emotional lift. Remember that you're not smiling at them in order to get something in return; you're not flirting, you're not hoping they will like you or admire you. This is just a little gift from you to the other person.

4. As you smile and look into their eyes, try to hold on to the idea that you started with: this person you're looking at has been an incredibly kind mother to you in a past life.

5. After you have caught their eye and given them a quick smile, break eye contact and move on. Remember to be careful not to

look at them for too long or do anything that might make them uncomfortable.

6. Try this out with at least five people during the course of the day. If you can, try it with every stranger you come in contact with all day—smile at them and think how grateful you are that they had been such a kind mother to you in an envisioned past life.

7. If you find that this exercise turns out to be a happy thing to do and that you meet with a good response from people, you might consider doing this for the rest your life. Can you imagine if the whole world went around smiling at strangers hoping to give them a spot of happiness? What a wonderful world that would be! In any case, we can practice stretching our own hearts and give a few random strangers a little bit of kindness.

 SHORT FORM

Look a stranger in the eyes, think that they had once been your kind mother, and smile warmly at them. Do this with as many strangers as possible.

24

Bearing Compassionate Witness to Suffering (Part 4)

THIS PRACTICE WILL HELP YOU:

▸ Increase awareness of and compassion for the suffering of others.

▸ Increase the ability to extend compassion regardless
of the scope of suffering.

▸ Increase the ability to extend compassion in hopeless
situations and regardless of outcomes.

▸ Expand your heart and mind to include animals as beings
for which you feel compassion.

Let me begin by giving you a heads-up that this is another difficult practice, along the lines of the one where you envisioned that you were a mother with no arms watching her child being carried away to swift and certain death in a river. Though difficult, this kind of compassion practice is time-tested; I included them because I trust their record of effectiveness. Please remember to particularly concentrate during the "First Invite Love In" meditation at the beginning of your practice—it will sustain you.

STEP ONE: Use the "First Invite Love In" meditation on page 15 before you begin this guided meditation.

STEP TWO: Please follow the instructions below for the central part of this compassion practice.

STEP THREE: Use the "Seal with a Vow and Rejoice" meditation on page 22 when you conclude this guided meditation.

1. Choose one place in the world where you know animals are finding their food supply dwindling to a perilous degree; imagine the terrain as it might be viewed from the perspective of an animal living in that area.

2. Envision a specific animal, perhaps one that you will find it easy to sympathize with, moving about in that habitat.

3. Imagine that this poor animal is too exhausted to search for food anymore. It's gotten to the point where, although its survival is at stake, it doesn't have the energy any longer to look for food.

4. See it having trouble moving. It has become so weak that every time it tries to move it stumbles and falls.

5. See it get to the point where it no longer attempts to even get up. And it's just lying on the ground, thirsty and hungry.

6. Imagine the physical sensations of starvation and thirst it experiences as its body fails. Perhaps it is also cold and wet. Or it might be too hot because it can't move into shade.

7. Now imagine it's aware that, lying there helpless and hopeless, it can't take care of itself and that it is vulnerable to attack. Just see this poor animal that is too tired to get up. It is looking around, aware that it's in danger. Predators might be coming close. It is frightened.

8. Just picture this poor, suffering animal, as it lies there and waits for death. Hours go by. Days go by. Finally, it succumbs.

9. Now think about the actual number of animals in this particular area of the world in just that one species that are likely suffering in this way.

10. Then think about all the animals of different kinds in this same part of the world that are starving, cold, or hot and are physically suffering, frightened, and dying.

11. If you can, think about another place in the world and a different kind of animal experiencing the same kind of trauma before death.

12. Go on over the globe thinking of different parts of the world where you know there have been floods or droughts that may have wiped out food supply or where people clearing or moving into areas have deprived the animals of their food supply. Or think of places in the oceans, lakes, or rivers: perhaps the waters have grown too warm, perhaps the coral are dying and so the fish that feed on the coral are dying, or perhaps the waters are too polluted to sustain healthy life.

13. Try to bring the entire planet into the forefront of your mind—all of these places around the world where animals are suffering—and hold all of them in your mind and your heart with kindness and compassion.

 SHORT FORM

Think of someplace in the world where you know that animals are having trouble finding enough food to survive. Imagine an animal too exhausted to search any more for food, stumbling to the ground and trying unsuccessfully to rise again. Imagine the days it lies there, thirsty and suffering from terrible hunger, until it succumbs to death. Imagine how helpless and hopeless it feels. Now think about the actual number of animals in this area that are suffering in this way. If you can, think about other places in the world and other kinds of animals that are also starving to death.

Connecting the Voice and Speech with Compassion

THIS PRACTICE WILL HELP YOU:

► Increase feelings of loving-kindness toward others.

► Increase awareness of the role of your voice and speech
as a means to express loving-kindness.

► Expand your heart to embrace and extend loving-kindness
to as many people as possible.

This practice is a variation of the earlier one where we envisioned a white light emanating from the center of our heads touching people and causing them to act with love and compassion.

STEP ONE: Use the "First Invite Love In" meditation on page 15 before you begin this guided meditation.

STEP TWO: Please follow the instructions below for the central part of this compassion practice.

STEP THREE: Use the "Seal with a Vow and Rejoice" meditation on page 22 when you conclude this guided meditation.

1. We'll begin first by locating a place in the center of your throat. Imagine there's an energy channel going from the top of your head straight down through your body. Imagine that, where the channel passes through the center of your throat, beautiful red light is emanating forth. This light has the ability to cause the people that it touches upon to speak from a place of love and peace.

2. First see this light extending out just a few inches around your neck. Extending and directing the light should be entirely effortless; imagine that the light is utterly limitless in its quantity and reach, and that all you have to do to extend its rays is picture it in your mind.

3. Now imagine that it extends out further: twenty or thirty feet. If you're inside, the light should pass through the walls of the building into the outside world. Try that.

4. Now imagine that the red light emanating from your throat

center reaches even further, and fans out, to the point where it encompasses your whole neighborhood.

5. Think of one particular neighbor who lives within a couple of blocks.

6. Envision the red light coming into them and then resonating in them, causing them to speak from a place of love and peace.

7. Take a minute for this. See the red light coming from you and your throat center. See it touching upon them; see their throat center begin to glow with red light. See them filling up with feelings of love and peace, and speaking from that place of love and peace.

8. Now try this thinking of another person in your neighborhood.

9. See a beautiful red light with a feeling of peaceful loving speech streaming out from your throat center.

10. Imagine it touches upon and enters the second person you thought of.

11. See something inside them transform and feelings of love and peace well up in them.

12. Finish by imagining that they start speaking to other people with love and peace conveyed through their voice and their words.

13. Now try to see all the people in your neighborhood lighting up with the loving red light that is emanating from your throat center.

14. See them all speaking with a feeling of love and peace that's conveyed through their voice and through the words they use.

15. Let's take it a step further. Locate that place in the center of your throat and imagine that there is red light extending out effortlessly and conveying a feeling of love and peace.

16. See the red light stretching out across your entire state and touching upon all the people in your state, filling them all with a feeling of love and peace that is expressed through their speech, the quality of their voice, and the words that they say.

17. Now start again with the visualization of red light that is extending out from your throat center.

18. This time imagine the light extends out across the entire country and lights up the throats of every single person all across the country, transforming their speech into something that carries with it feelings of love and peace.

19. Now let's stretch this visualization out to the entire planet. A beautiful red light with feelings of love and peace extends out from your throat center.

20. The red light travels out and around the entire planet, touching upon the throat centers of every single human being on the planet, transforming their speech so that the quality of their voices and the things they say convey love and peace. See the entire planet and every single human being with beautiful red light extending out from their throat centers, speaking from a place of love and peace. Wouldn't that sound nice?

 Short Form

Imagine a red light in the center of your throat that sends out rays of love and peace in all directions. Imagine the red light extends a few inches around your body. Continue extending the light until it encompasses your neighborhood, then your whole state, then your country, and finally until it bathes the entire earth in red rays and everyone on earth speaks from a place of love and peace.

26

THINKING OF ANIMALS AS KIND MOTHERS

THIS PRACTICE WILL HELP YOU:

▶ Increase trust of others by creating a sense of kinship.

▶ Increase love for others by creating a sense of gratitude.

▶ Reduce feelings of divisiveness and "us vs. them."

▶ Expand your heart and mind to include animals in your
feelings of compassion and loving-kindness.

In this practice we're going to work with the foundation practice of
thinking of others as having been your kind mothers in imagined past
lives, but this time venturing outside the human realm and imagining
that an animal could have been your mother in an envisioned past life.
Let me remind you again that this is just a means to train our minds to
have greater compassion toward all living creatures, people and animals
alike, and doesn't mean that you necessarily believe in reincarnation.

STEP ONE: Use the "First Invite Love In" meditation on page 15 before you begin this guided meditation.

STEP TWO: Please follow the instructions below for the central part of this compassion practice.

STEP THREE: Use the "Seal with a Vow and Rejoice" meditation on page 22 when you conclude this guided meditation.

1. Bring to mind a particular individual animal that you like very much. It could be an animal that is or was a pet and so was part of your life. It could be an animal that you've seen in the surrounding area. It could be a friend's pet or a farm animal. Or you could think of an animal that you've seen in a movie or on television. Just bring to mind an animal that you have particularly warm feelings for.

2. Then imagine that there is such a thing as a past life and that in a past life the essence of this animal, its soul, was actually your mother. As your mother, think that this animal was the kindest, most loving, and caring mother to you possible.

3. Think that in another lifetime this animal took care of you in the most loving and ideal fashion possible. It made sure that you had everything that you needed to be happy, nurtured, supported, and protected. All of that happened because they

loved you so much and they were so careful, kind, and giving to you when you were a child.

4. Imagine how grateful you would have been as a child to have such a kind and loving mother. See the love that you would have extended back to this mother who—in their essence, in their soul—was actually this animal. Take a little time to try that out in your mind.

5. Next try this visualization out while thinking about other animals that you've seen in your neighborhood—birds, squirrels, or farm animals, depending on where you live—one individual at a time.

6. Imagine that in a past life each animal wasn't an animal. It was a human being. In fact, it was your mother and was incredibly kind to you and took care of you. It did everything that the most perfect mother would do for you.

7. Think how loved and protected you would have felt.

8. See how grateful you would have been to this mother who is also, in its essence, the animal in your neighborhood.

9. Try that sequence out, thinking of different animals in your neighborhood.

10. Then stretch your heart and mind wider, and think that all the animals in your neighborhood in a one mile radius have been your kind mothers in a past life. Imagine that the squirrels, birds, mice, and insects that surround you were, every single one of them, in a past life the kindest and most loving and protective mothers possible.

11. See and feel how grateful you would have been to all of them for having been so kind, loving, and protective of you as a child.

12. Next think that all the animals and creatures in your state—insects, wildlife, fish, and birds—have been your kind mothers in a past life.

13. Think that, as your mothers, they were incredibly loving to you, watching out to make sure that you had everything you needed to be strong, healthy, and protected. They looked on you with fondness and love.

14. Imagine how grateful you would have been to them and how much you would have loved these mothers in return. Imagine all these kind mothers all over your state and the love and gratitude that you feel in return.

15. Then extend this visualization in your mind to encompass every single animal, insect, and creature of the water, of the air, and underground in the entire country and think that all of them have been your kind mother in a past life—watching out for you, loving you, holding you, feeding you, and cleaning you with the greatest of care and kindness.

16. Think how grateful you would have been to each and every one of them in all of these lifetimes. Think how much love you would have had for all these wildlife mothers all over your country.

17. Now open your heart and mind further to embrace the whole world including the oceans, inland seas, lakes, and rivers. Think that everything that flies in the air, swims in the water, crawls on the ground, or burrows through the earth—every single one of those creatures has been your kindest, kindest, most loving, caring, protective, supportive, and nurturing mother possible.

18. Imagine how you would have felt love and how grateful you would have been in return. Think how much you would have loved each and every one of those animals in each and every lifetime for having been such a kind mother to you.

 SHORT FORM

Think about a particular animal you know and like. Imagine that in a past life this animal had been the most loving and caring mother to you conceivable. Imagine that this animal made every sacrifice possible to shield you from danger, comfort you in sadness, and attend to your every need. Then think about how grateful you would have been when you were a child to this animal for taking such kind care of you. Now try this sequence thinking about all the animals, including the smallest life forms, in your neighborhood, state, then your country, and finally throughout the entire earth.

27

IMAGINING SHARING THE SOURCE OF YOUR GOOD FORTUNE WITH OTHERS

THIS PRACTICE WILL HELP YOU:

▸ Increase loving-kindness toward others.

▸ Increase feelings of generosity.

▸ Reduce attachment to possessions.

▸ Overcome or reduce selfishness and the implicit view
of life as a zero-sum game.

STEP ONE: Use the "First Invite Love In" meditation on page 15 before you begin this guided meditation.

STEP TWO: Please follow the instructions below for the central part of this compassion practice.

STEP THREE: Use the "Seal with a Vow and Rejoice" meditation on page 22 when you conclude this guided meditation.

1. Imagine that you could take the source of all of your past, future, and current good fortune that has brought about all your health, success, money, happiness, and peace of mind—essentially anything good that has happened in the past, is with you now, and will be with you in the future—all your good luck, and put an exact replica of that power in a box.

2. Next imagine your mother. You can either think of your mother as she is in this life or, if that is problematic for some reason, you can imagine that in a past life she was the most kind, wonderful, loving, and caring mother.

3. Now imagine yourself giving this box that contains the essence of all your good luck to your mother. Remember that, in this visualization, giving away your good fortune does not adversely affect you. You will not be poorer or lonelier or more ill. You have simply done a great thing for your mother. See her receive the box, and know that she will have greater good fortune for the rest of her life.

4. Next see yourself giving another box that also contains a replica of the source of your good fortune to your father. You can imagine, if you want, your father as he is now, or you can imagine that in a past life he was the kindest, most loving, and caring mother possible.

5. Imagine that as a result of receiving the box your father has great good fortune.

6. See how happy he is; see how the rest of his life will be happier, healthier, successful, and more peaceful.

7. Then go through this visualization thinking one by one of the rest of your family—your brothers and sisters, your aunts and uncles, cousins, grandparents, great-grandparents, your husband or wife.

8. Next see yourself going to your boyfriend or girlfriend and all your good friends with this box filled with great good fortune. In every case imagine that in their essence they are the same person who was the kindest and most loving mother to you in a past life. Give them the box. See them take it and see their happiness. Look forward in the future and imagine that their lives take a turn for the better in every aspect.

9. Now think of a person you don't like—a person with whom you've had some difficulties. They make you irritated, annoyed, or worse. Now imagine that they've been the kindest, most loving mother to you in a past life. This is who they are in their essence. Now see yourself giving them the box of good fortune. See them become very happy and their lives taking a turn for the better in the future.

10. Stretch your mind and heart wider; see yourself bestowing this box of good fortune on everyone in your neighborhood. They have all been your kind mother in a past life. See them all becoming very happy and having greater success, wealth, health, peace of mind, and happiness in the future. See that for your whole neighborhood.

11. Then extend this visualization out to your state. Hundreds of thousands or millions of boxes of good fortune stream out from you to every person in the state. Every person in the state is very happy and will experience good fortune in every way.

12. Now think of the entire country and imagine that every single human being in the country has been your very kind mother in a past life. See yourself giving each and every one of them the box filled with a replica of the source of all of the good fortune that you've had in this life. See how happy they are to receive it. And imagine that everyone in the country as a result of having this box filled with your good fortune goes on to experience greater happiness, success, power, fame, and peace of mind in the future.

13. End by thinking of every person on the planet. Think that they have all been your very kind mothers in a past life. They've all been very loving, protective, and supportive of you. Imagine

that quite naturally you were very grateful as a child and loved them in return.

14. Now take this box that is filled with a replica of the source of everything good that has happened to you in the past, present, and future and give it to them. You lose nothing by doing so. In fact, your own store of good fortune increases by virtue of doing this.

15. See everyone on the planet very pleased to have received the box and see them in their future lives all experiencing greater luck in everything they do and having greater happiness, more money, stronger health, and better peace of mind.

 ## Short Form

Imagine you could take the source of all of your past and future good fortune—the source of all your health, success, money, happiness, and peace of mind—and make a replica of it that you put in box. Now imagine giving this box to your mother so that she will have good fortune. Then to your father, to the rest of your family and friends, to people you don't like, to everyone in your neighborhood, your state, your country, and ultimately to everyone in the world.

28

BREATHE IN WITH COMPASSION, BREATHE OUT WITH LOVING-KINDNESS (PART 2)

THIS PRACTICE WILL HELP YOU:

▸ Increase awareness of the suffering of others and aspiration to relieve them of that suffering.

▸ Increase feelings of loving-kindness toward others and an aspiration to contribute to their happiness in life.

▸ Create an association in your mind between a basic life function (breathing) and feelings of compassion and loving-kindness.

This practice is a variation on the theme of the second practice in the book. In this version, we are going to imagine that we are able to relieve people of mental suffering created by cruel or unkind things that have been said or done to them by breathing into ourselves all those painful memories and the impact that they've had on their minds, and then beaming into them a healing white light as we exhale. Remember that inhaling the smoke and emitting the light is not at all painful to you; you relieve them of their burden without assuming the burden yourself.

STEP ONE: Use the "First Invite Love In" meditation on page 15 before you begin this guided meditation.

STEP TWO: Please follow the instructions below for the central part of this compassion practice.

STEP THREE: Use the "Seal with a Vow and Rejoice" meditation on page 22 when you conclude this guided meditation.

1. Begin by thinking of one individual who you imagine in a past life was a loving and kind mother to you, and to whom you feel immense love and gratitude.

2. Now imagine that whenever something cruel, unkind, or hurtful happened to this person it left a register in their minds, like a dark spot. Think that they not only experienced the pain in the moment when it was inflicted, but they have an ongoing memory of it that negatively alters the way they feel about themselves and about the world.

3. Now breathe in, and picture that dark spot dissolving into smoke as you draw it out of them and into yourself, where it is rendered harmless.

4. Now imagine a storehouse of goodness within yourself that has been created as a result of all the good things that you've done in your life. Exhale, and think that from this beautiful golden storehouse a brilliant white light effortlessly radiates out and touches this person, filling them with a lasting feeling of peace and happiness.

5. Now bring the entire planet to the forefront of your mind and see it dotted with billions of points of light representing individuals all over the surface of the globe. See all the lights and have a general awareness of all human beings all over the planet.

6. Then imagine that all those points of light, those human beings, had been the kindest, most caring, and loving mothers to you in past lives, and that you feel tremendous gratitude and love in return for their kindnesses in those past lives. Just take a minute and see if you can get a sense of kinship with all human beings all over the planet.

7. Imagine that all the people all over the world, all those loving mothers, have dark spots in their mindsets representing unhappy experiences and unkind or cruel things that have happened to them.

8. Now breathe in, and envision that all of those spots of pain lift off their minds like black soot or gray mist, leaving their minds clean and pure. See it all streaming off, all over the planet.

9. Imagine that it comes harmlessly into you.

10. Then visualize that from the storehouse of merit within you a brilliant white light with the intentionality of giving others a sense of peace and happiness wells up within you.

11. Exhale, and imagine that the white light extends out without any effort on your part and without depleting you. It just naturally extends out and touches upon every single one of those individuals across the planet that you are envisioning has actually been your kind mother in a past life.

12. See all these people experience a wonderful sense of peace and happiness as the light touches them. Think that it makes a lasting impression on their minds. This all happens on the exhalation of your breath.

13. Continue to work on this exercise until you get to the point where you can do it following along with the natural rhythm of your breath—you take in the pain and suffering as you inhale and you send out healing white light as you exhale.

Imagine that you have the power to relieve people of the mental suffering they experience as a result of the cruel and unkind things that have been done to them. Imagine that you can take away the memory and impact of those terrible experiences by breathing them into yourself in the form of black smoke or mist. Then imagine that, from your store of merit and virtue built up from the good things you have done and thought during your life, you send out peace and happiness to all living beings by infusing them with brilliant white light as you breathe out. Repeat this as many times as possible.

Expanding the Heart to Have Compassion for People Who Have Been Unfair or Hurt You

THIS PRACTICE WILL HELP YOU:

▸ Increase awareness of the suffering of others and aspiration to relieve them of that suffering.

▸ Increase trust of others by creating a sense of kinship.

▸ Increase love for others by creating a sense of gratitude.

▸ Reduce feelings of divisiveness and "us vs. them."

▸ Diminish feelings of anger and bitterness.

▸ Diminish holding grudges.

▸ Overcome an egocentric view of others.

Remember that this and all other practices in this book are compassion exercises for your benefit; this is not a prayer and it is not magic and will not actually change anyone's behavior but your own.

STEP ONE: Use the "First Invite Love In" meditation on page 15 before you begin this guided meditation.

STEP TWO: Please follow the instructions below for the central part of this compassion practice.

STEP THREE: Use the "Seal with a Vow and Rejoice" meditation on page 22 when you conclude this guided meditation.

1. Bring to mind someone who has done an injustice to you that still makes you feel hurt or angry when you think about it. Take a little time to think of this person and to remember the situation—remember both how you felt about it at the time and over time.

2. Now set aside any desire that you might have for remedy, restitution, revenge, or justice. Take all of those kinds of thoughts and put them aside for a while. They don't do you any good anyway, and in this case they'll really get in the way of the compassion practice that we're about to do for your own benefit.

3. Then think of the person as having been the kindest, most loving, and most caring mother to you in an imaginary past life. Feel how grateful you would have been in return and how much you would wish that everything wonderful would happen for them. I know this is a stretch, but it's a necessary

foundation to work with this practice and it will be helpful and beneficial for you to do it.

4. Imagine that in this current life this person experienced many unkind and difficult things. Maybe people were cruel to them, neglected them, or were unfair to them. All of that registered on their minds, demoralized them, perhaps lowered their self-esteem, and made them angry or unreasonable. Perhaps this is why they were hurtful to you. As a result of these terrible things, this person who was once such a kind mother to you has a diminished capacity for a happy and peaceful life.

5. Take a little time to try to see all of this and feel compassion for the difficult experiences this person has had in the past and will probably have in the future. Remember that, at their core, this person has been the kindest mother possible to you in a past life. Then they came into this life and unfortunate circum-stances led them to develop a personality such that they do hurtful, angry, and negative things to other people, which only compounds their future problems and diminishes their chance of attaining peace and happiness.

6. Now imagine that you have the ability to remove this negativity from their mindstream and replace it with compassion and loving-kindness. See something like a dark web on their mind

that represents negative behavior patterns that are likely to lead to more problems and unhappy experiences in their lives.

7. Imagine that you miraculously lift away that dark web, leaving them a clean slate of mind imbued with compassion and loving-kindness.

8. Imagine that they become kind and compassionate to other people for the rest of their lives. Because of your miraculous ability to lift negativity out of them and replace it with loving-kindness, peace, and compassion, they will never again treat anyone as they did you. See them in that way for a little while.

9. If you can, go through this process with each and every person that you believe has acted badly toward you or has hurt or been unfair to you in some way.

10. In each case begin by thinking that the person was your kind mother in a past life but in this life they had difficult experiences and so developed a personality such that they behaved toward you in a negative fashion.

11. Next imagine you lift that negativity out of them and replace it with compassion, peace, and loving-kindness.

12. See them go forward in life in a very different manner—feeling peaceful and happy and behaving with kindness and compassion toward others.

 ## Short Form

Think about someone who has done an injustice to you that still makes you hurt or angry when you think about it. Then imagine the negativity that is in this person's mind and the ways that this negativity is hurting their chance to have a happy and peaceful life. Now imagine that you can take this negativity out of their mindstream and replace it with compassion and loving-kindness. If you can, think this way about each and every person you feel has acted badly toward you.

Bearing Compassionate Witness
to Suffering (Part 5)

THIS PRACTICE WILL HELP YOU:

▶ Increase awareness of and compassion for the suffering of others.

▶ Increase the ability to extend compassion regardless
of the scope of suffering.

▶ Increase the ability to extend compassion in hopeless
situations and regardless of outcomes.

▶ Expand your heart and mind to include animals as beings
for which you feel compassion.

This is another one of the practices where we open our hearts even
further by fully contemplating the suffering of another living being. In
this case we will be contemplating animals that are suffering because
of their treatment by human beings—suffering from which there is no
hope of relief except for death. Tragically, there are many, many ways

that this can occur. Before you begin, remember to perform very carefully the "First Invite Love In" meditation to gather strength.

STEP ONE: Use the "First Invite Love In" meditation on page 15 before you begin this guided meditation.

STEP TWO: Please follow the instructions below for the central part of this compassion practice.

STEP THREE: Use the "Seal with a Vow and Rejoice" meditation on page 22 when you conclude this guided meditation.

1. Choose one kind of circumstance where animals are mistreated by human beings. Unfortunately there are many to choose from: beasts of burden that are compelled to work beyond their endurance; animals being raised for food in horrible conditions that make their lives fearful and brief; animals raised for sports that are abused during their training and slaughtered when they no longer win. Choose one that is particularly poignant to you.

2. Now think of an individual animal in that situation. Take some time to imagine the worst circumstances in this kind of situation unfolding. See it from the animal's perspective. See the animal suffering through physical pain, fear, or hunger.

Perhaps its master yells harshly at it or beats it until it bleeds. Allow the entire scene to unfold before your eyes, all the suffering and the horror, without turning away.

3. Then think about all the animals in the same kind of circumstance all over the world at this moment in time. Just imagine the sheer numbers of them. Perhaps you can see them as points of light dotting the planet. Recognize the extent of suffering that is being experienced by animals at the hands of people all over the world right now.

4. Stretch this awareness backward and forward in time.

5. Next expand your heart and mind to include animals' suffering in all the other categories of abuse and mistreatment that you can think of. Just hold that in the forefront of your mind and in your heart for a moment.

Think about a place in the world where animals are badly mistreated by people who use them for labor. Think about a particular beast of burden that is worn out and too tired to do what its master wants no matter how hard it tries. Then think about the animal being harshly yelled at and beaten until its skin is cut and it bleeds. Now multiply this situation by the number of animals you think are probably suffering like that in this place at this very moment. Then if you can, think about animals in other parts of the world that are suffering terribly in the same way with no hope of relief except their death.

Taking Compassion into Daily Life: Imagining Generosity toward Strangers

THIS PRACTICE WILL HELP YOU:

▸ Increase loving-kindness toward others.

▸ Increase feelings of generosity.

▸ Reduce attachment to possessions.

▸ Overcome or reduce selfishness and the implicit
view of life as a zero-sum game.

▸ Take the practice loving-kindness toward others
into the realm of daily life.

▸ Take the practice of feeling greater trust, kinship, and gratitude
toward others into the realm of daily life.

This is one of the practices that you'll be doing out in the real world
rather than visualizing on your own. You will be working with the

imagery from this practice in your mind as you look at strangers throughout the day. As always, we don't want to make other people feel uncomfortable while we are working on compassion practices, so it will help to spend some time early in the day to prepare yourself well. This way, when you're out in the world, the practice will immediately come to mind when you look at someone so that you can work through it quickly without making the person wonder what is going on.

This is also a practice where it might be helpful to remember that this is merely a compassion exercise for you, and will not affect the real-life fortunes of anyone around you or your own.

STEP ONE: Use the "First Invite Love In" meditation on page 15 before you begin this guided meditation.

STEP TWO: Please follow the instructions below for the central part of this compassion practice.

STEP THREE: Use the "Seal with a Vow and Rejoice" meditation on page 22 when you conclude this guided meditation.

1. Begin by preparing yourself to view each stranger as if they had been the kindest, most loving, and caring mother to you in an envisioned past life. Think that in their essence they are not a stranger to you at all but were once a wonderful mother to you.

Experience yourself feeling tremendous gratitude and love in return for all their past kindness and care.

2. Next imagine that you give this stranger everything that you own. Imagine that you give them the key to your home; that you give them your car; you give them all your belongings, all your money, and all your assets. For the purposes of this visualization imagine that there are no real consequences to giving these things away. This generosity won't hurt you at all; you can simply be delighted at the opportunity to repay this person for their past kindness to you.

3. Let's review the sequence of visualization and thoughts. First just look at the person and envision they have been your kind mother in a past life and you feel grateful in return.

4. Then see yourself giving them the five things you most treasure, one by one. Or, if you prefer, you can envision everything you own packed in a truckload. See yourself giving all this to the person.

5. Finish by mentally and emotionally moving on from this thought without regret or clinging.

6. Try this exercise out with at least five strangers during the course of the day ahead.

 Short Form

Look at a stranger and imagine giving them everything you own: the keys to your home, your car, all your belongings, and all your money and assets. Think like this for as many strangers as possible. (It won't hurt you to just imagine this. It doesn't cost you anything really. It is the thought that counts, but it is surprisingly hard to entertain this idea as a thought even though it has no real consequences.)

Overcoming Jealousy and Envy to Rejoice for the Emotional Happiness of Others

THIS PRACTICE WILL HELP YOU:

▸ Increase compassion for and loving-kindness toward others.

▸ Increase ability to rejoice for others.

▸ Decrease envy and jealousy.

▸ Overcome or reduce egotism and the implicit
view of life as a zero-sum game.

▸ Expand the heart to embrace the greatest number of people
possible and wish for their happiness.

STEP ONE: Use the "First Invite Love In" meditation on page 15 before you begin this guided meditation.

STEP TWO: Please follow the instructions below for the central part of this compassion practice.

STEP THREE: Use the "Seal with a Vow and Rejoice" meditation on page 22 when you conclude this guided meditation.

1. Think of someone you know or know of who feels lonely, someone who experiences a lot of pain and sadness because they wish they had a loving partner in their lives. Perhaps this is someone who's recently gone through a divorce, broken up with someone, or has never been able to have a relationship. This would be someone who has been alone for a long time and you know that they've been sad and they've been yearning for companionship, love, romance, and everything else that comes along with a loving partner in your life.

2. Bring this person into the forefront of your mind and then imagine that someone kind and wonderful comes into their life and they fall completely and madly in love. Imagine that this love is reciprocated. They have a fantastic relationship. It is clear that they're going to spend the rest of their lives together supporting each other and loving each other. It's a real dream come true for them.

3. Imagine the love, joy, and bliss this person feels now that they experience a deep and secure love. Try to get into the mind of this person and see how they would feel, as love from their partner showers upon them, knowing that they had the love of their life by their side.

4. Now, after imagining the happiness that person must be experiencing, feel yourself rejoice and be happy for them. Try to keep all thoughts of your own circumstance regarding love relationships out of the picture. Focus entirely on celebrating without reserve that your friend or the person you are thinking of is well loved. Take a little time to envision that.

5. Now estimate how many people in your neighborhood are uncoupled and are unhappy about it. See them as a group, and then imagine that they all find their soulmates and are incredibly happy. They are all experiencing the most perfect romance imaginable. See everybody being happy.

6. Feel happy for them. Rejoice for them.

7. Open your heart and mind further to imagine that all the lonely people in your whole state, all the people who wish they were in a relationship, get matched up romantically with someone who's completely crazy about them, adores them, and is supportive of them. Imagine these circles of loving unions across the state.

8. Feel happy for everyone. Remember that their romantic situations do not in any way affect your own prospects or circumstances.

9. Then stretch this visualization out to the entire country. Imagine that all the lonely hearts in the country who have been yearning and pining for true love meet their perfect partner. It's clear they're all going to have long-lasting, ideal, and loving relationships. See the country dotted with these adoring couples.

10. Be happy for them all and rejoice.

11. Now imagine that all the people in every single country on the planet who have been unhappily alone all find their perfect romantic partner. Visualize that they all are experiencing the true joy of being the object of another person's affection and devotion. Feel how they feel.

12. Feel happy for them and imagine the planet full of these people who are in loving relationships.

Think about someone you know who feels lonely and experiences a lot of pain and sadness because they wish they had a loving partner in their lives. Now imagine that someone kind and wonderful comes into their lives, someone who immediately loves them deeply and wants to spend the rest of their lives together with them. Imagine the love, joy, and bliss this person feels now that they experience a deep and secure love. Imagine this happens to all the lonely people you know. Then it happens to all the lonely people in your neighborhood, state, country, and the world.

33

Taking Compassion into Daily Life: Imbuing Simple Greetings with Compassion

THIS PRACTICE WILL HELP YOU:

► Create an association in your mind between simple daily greetings and the expression of compassion.

► Take the practice of compassion into the realm of daily life.

► Take the practice of feeling greater trust, kinship, and gratitude toward others into the realm of daily life.

► Increase awareness of and compassion for the suffering of others.

This is another practice that you will be using throughout the day in relation to perfect strangers. It's important to mentally prepare yourself at the start of your day by practicing the "First Invite Love In" meditation.

STEP ONE: Use the "First Invite Love In" meditation on page 15 before you begin this guided meditation.

STEP TWO: Please follow the instructions below for the central part of this compassion practice.

STEP THREE: Use the "Seal with a Vow and Rejoice" meditation on page 22 when you conclude this guided meditation.

1. Look for a person on the street who seems sad, hurt, or upset. You don't need to know or confirm that this is actually the case; it is just your perception that the person is not at peace and not feeling completely happy. Something has thrown them off, made them uncomfortable, made them angry, or somewhat fearful.

2. Visualize that at their essence this person is not actually a stranger to you. They were once your wonderful and loving mother. Try to feel as if you share that closest bond: between a mother and a child.

3. Now make eye contact with them, smile warmly at them, and wish them a good day out loud. Make sure that they can see and hear you. Release any expectation that this will have a significant impact on their life and any hope on your part that they will like or admire you as a result of the interaction. You

are merely showing them that you've noticed them and wishing them a little joy.

4. Do this with at least five people during the day ahead.

 ## SHORT FORM

Look for someone on the street or in a public place who seems sad, hurt, or upset. Look them in the eyes, smile warmly at them, and wish them a good day. Do this for as many people as possible.

34

BEARING COMPASSIONATE WITNESS
TO SUFFERING (PART 6)

THIS PRACTICE WILL HELP YOU:

▸ Increase awareness of and compassion for the suffering of others.

▸ Increase the ability to extend compassion regardless
of the scope of suffering.

▸ Increase the ability to extend compassion in hopeless situations
and regardless of outcomes.

▸ Expand your heart and mind to include animals as beings
for which you feel compassion.

This is the last of the set of compassion practices where we open our
hearts wide to allow ourselves to witness, comprehend, and feel compassion for the suffering of other living beings. In this final exercise we
are going to fully contemplate the difficult life circumstances of wildlife. Please pay special attention to the "First Invite Love In" meditation

before you begin so as to gather the support and strength needed to fully engage with this practice.

STEP ONE: Use the "First Invite Love In" meditation on page 15 before you begin this guided meditation.

STEP TWO: Please follow the instructions below for the central part of this compassion practice.

STEP THREE: Use the "Seal with a Vow and Rejoice" meditation on page 22 when you conclude this guided meditation.

1. Think of a bird, squirrel, or some other kind of animal that you are pretty familiar with that lives outside on its own. We are going to think in some detail about what its life is really like.

2. Think about how it tries to find food every day and that its food supply is not guaranteed. Imagine that animal's struggle. Think about what it might be like for it to travel to a place that has been a food source in the past only to find nothing left. It may be difficult to find water, too.

3. Imagine what it is like for the animal to compete with others for food. Perhaps it has to fight off aggressive animals that are also just trying to survive. It has to watch its back throughout the whole process of eating; animals that are stronger will try

to push it aside. Imagine how it feels when it is prevented from getting as much food as it needs.

4. Think about what it is like for this animal when it searches for shelter for the first time on its own, without its mother. See it searching out a home, alone and anxious.

5. Think about what it is like for the animal when others are competing for the same place. Even after it has found a home, it may need to defend it against others.

6. Imagine the animal's experience if the natural elements destroy its shelter. Perhaps heavy rain or snow ruin it; the animal is now wet or cold and must either rebuild or replace its home.

7. Think about what it is like for the animal when it grows into maturity and it has to compete to mate. It may be a brutal experience. Imagine what it is like for the animal to be prevented from mating.

8. If it succeeds in mating and is involved with rearing its young, imagine what it is like for the animal to defend its young against attacks from predators. Imagine what it is like for the animal to be constantly wary, watching for signs, sounds, shadows, and

the behavior of other animals that might indicate that there's a danger.

9. Imagine the experience of the animal as it gets old and weak and has a harder and harder time fending for itself, protecting its resting place and home, and fighting for food. It will slowly lose ground in this battle and become even weaker as a result.

10. Think about the very end of life for any animal living in the wild. It is not likely to be a pleasant one. It may grow weak to the point where it can no longer take care of itself and then perhaps slowly starve to death or die of thirst. Imagine what it might be like for the animal to be unable to get up to find food to take care of itself. In this weak condition it will be aware that it's vulnerable to attack and likely to feel quite frightened. Alternatively, before it weakens it may come under attack, which may or may not be a quick and easy death. Imagine the animal's experience when it undergoes a painful, frightening fight with physical pain and a lingering death.

11. All in all, the life of any animal living in the wild has inherently a great deal of suffering from start to finish. Let yourself contemplate this fully with compassion. Think about the life-cycle of an animal and all the things it has to do to survive and the constant threats it lives under. Allow yourself to fully see

the precarious life, the danger, and the suffering that wildlife encounter during the course of their lives.

12. Do this for as many kinds of animals as possible.

 ## Short Form

Look at a bird or a squirrel living outside. Think about what its life is like. Think about how it has to find food every day. Think about it trying to find shelter when it is cold, windy, and raining or snowing. Think about how other animals chase it away from food it needs and the place where it wants to rest. Think about how it will eventually die through accident, being attacked by other animals, through sickness, or starvation. Do this for as many animals as possible.

Transforming Our Own Suffering into a Compassionate Impulse

THIS PRACTICE WILL HELP YOU:

▸ Make an association between one's own personal hardships
and the aspiration to relieve others of suffering.

▸ Increase awareness of and compassion for the suffering of others.

▸ Overcome or reduce the influence of anger or bitterness
on your ability to feel compassion for others.

In this practice we are going to wish that other people would not have to endure the same kinds of hardships and difficult life situations that we have gone through. Remember, again, that these are simply compassion exercises and will not actually bring you more suffering or affect anyone else.

Step One: Use the "First Invite Love In" meditation on page 15 before you begin this guided meditation.

STEP TWO: Please follow the instructions below for the central part of this compassion practice.

STEP THREE: Use the "Seal with a Vow and Rejoice" meditation on page 22 when you conclude this guided meditation.

1. Think of a terrible situation that you have experienced or are currently experiencing.

2. Think of someone that you care about. Imagine, as always, that they've been your kind mother in an envisioned past life and that you feel tremendous gratitude and love for them in return.

3. Imagine that you could make a bargain with the powers that be where you would say that, since you are enduring or have endured this pain, let your pain represent and substitute for the same kind of pain in this person that you care about. Because you are suffering, let no one else suffer. Imagine that that is the deal you have struck.

4. Then think of another difficult situation you have endured in your life, something that's specific to you, and that's real and painful.

5. Think of a distant acquaintance, someone you don't know very well. Someone you feel neutral about. Imagine that in

their essence in an envisioned past life they were the kindest, most loving, and wonderful mother to you. They took wonderful care of you and you feel tremendous gratitude and love in return. Imagine that there was a very deep bond between you.

6. In regard for that bond between you, and your love and gratitude, think that you wish to spare them from having to experience the second kind of difficult life experience. Make the wish or the aspiration that this person would be spared from ever under any circumstances having to go through what you are going through or have gone through in the past. Wish that by virtue of your having experienced this kind of suffering and hardship that you can take it on for them. Think about that.

7. Think of a third specific difficult life circumstance that is or has been painful, sad, or difficult for you.

8. Now bring to mind someone that you don't like. Think of someone who's been difficult to deal with, someone who has perhaps been mean or unfair to you. Imagine that they have been the kindest, most loving, and wonderful mother to you in an envisioned past life. You know by now how to think through that scenario to the point where it has real meaning for you. Think that the essence, the soul, or the core of this person is actually that kind mother for whom you had such love and gratitude.

9. With that in mind, wish that they could be spared ever experiencing the same kind of difficulty, sadness, and pain that you have experienced in the past or are experiencing now. Wish that you could take this on for them and that your suffering could spare them from the same experience.

10. In the future, if you can, any time that you are experiencing something difficult in your life, make the aspiration that others would be spared from having to go through the same sort of pain that you are experiencing. In reality, you wouldn't wish this kind of suffering upon anyone else—you really would wish that you could spare them—we just don't normally stop to take the opportunity to think this way in the moment. Counterintuitive as it may seem, you'll find that doing so actually eases your own pain and suffering.

 SHORT FORM

Think about something sad that has happened in your life. Now imagine that, by virtue of your having experienced that sad event, you could prevent any other person on earth from ever having to experience the same kind of unfortunate event. Imagine this first with regard to people you care deeply about. Then imagine you could save people you don't like from suffering in this way.

BREATHE IN WITH COMPASSION, BREATHE OUT WITH LOVING-KINDNESS (PART 3)

THIS PRACTICE WILL HELP YOU:

▶ Increase awareness of the suffering of others and develop
the aspiration to relieve them of that suffering.

▶ Increase awareness of negative thought patterns
and actions as a source of suffering.

▶ Increase feelings of loving-kindness toward others and develop
the aspiration to contribute to their happiness in life.

▶ Create an association in your mind between a basic life function
(breathing) and feelings of compassion and loving-kindness.

This is the final variation of the second practice in the series, "Breathe In with Compassion, Breathe Out with Loving-Kindness," where we envision inhaling into ourselves suffering or negativity from other people's minds and then, exhaling, imagine a brilliant white light coming out of us from a never-ending source that infuses the people it touches with feelings of peace, love, and happiness. In this version we're going to be imagining that we are relieving other people of the traces of negativity in their minds that they have created through negative things that they have done, said, or thought. This kind of negative action leaves a record in the mind that can create (or reinforce) patterns of negative behavior that then are likely to bring more pain and distress to the person. Remember that we will imagine that this smoke or grey mist of negativity will not in any way burden us, and that sending out the rays of healing light does not exhaust us; we will be drawing upon an endless source of peace, love, and happiness from our spiritual support figure.

STEP ONE: Use the "First Invite Love In" meditation on page 15 before you begin this guided meditation.

STEP TWO: Please follow the instructions below for the central part of this compassion practice.

STEP THREE: Use the "Seal with a Vow and Rejoice" meditation on page 22 when you conclude this guided meditation.

1. Think of someone you know who has said, thought, or done something negative. Bring them clearly into the forefront of your mind.

2. Now imagine that this negativity has left a record like a spot of black soot on their mind.

3. Now inhale, and picture yourself breathing in all traces of negativity from their mind, so that the spot dissolves and comes into you like harmless black smoke or grey mist.

4. Then exhale and imagine a brilliant white light extending out from you that has the ability infuse a person it touches with peace, love, and happiness without depleting you in any way.

5. Visualize the person being infused with the white light and see them feeling peaceful, happy, and loving.

6. Let's try three more rounds of this. Breathe in and see the negativity lifting off of them and coming into you.

7. Breathe out and see white light coming out of you, touching upon them, and making them very happy and peaceful.

8. Again, breathe in and see the negativity coming out of them like black smoke and coming into you.

9. Breathe out and imagine that white light extends out from you and touches them, filling them with peace, love, and happiness.

10. Try that one last time. Breathe in and see negativity come off of them and into you.

11. Breathe out and visualize that white light touches upon them, making them very happy and peaceful.

12. Now think about all human beings on the earth. See the globe of the planet in your mind. Visualize points of light representing billions of people all over the earth where every point of light is mottled with some black marks that represent records in their minds of negative things they have done, said, or thought.

13. We will do three rounds of breathing where you imagine that the negativity comes off of them as you inhale—negativity from billions of minds all over the planet—and streams into you, yet it doesn't burden you. When you exhale see brilliant white light extending out from an endless source of happiness within you and touching upon all those billions of bright lights, making them light up even brighter with feelings of happiness, peace, and love.

14. Inhale, breathing negativity in . . .

15. And exhale with the white light of peace, love, and happiness going out to them.

16. Again, see the black dots of negativity on everyone all over the planet.

17. Inhale and see that rise up and off of them into you.

18. Then exhale happiness in a bright white light that extends out to all of those points of light that now glow even brighter with happiness, peace, and love.

19. One last time, see the negativity in people like black dots on the points of white light that represent them.

20. Inhale all that.

21. Then exhale happiness in a brilliant white light that goes out all over the planet to the people who light up even brighter with peace, love, and happiness.

Imagine that you have the power to relieve people of the negativity they have created in their minds as a result of having thought, said, or done cruel or unkind things to other people. Imagine that you can take away the memory and impact of those negative thoughts, words, and actions by breathing them into yourself in the form of black smoke or mist. Then imagine that, from your store of merit and virtue built up from the good things you have done and thought during your life, you send out peace and happiness to all living beings by infusing them with brilliant white light as you breathe out. Repeat this as many times as possible.

Connecting the Mind and Thoughts with Compassion

THIS PRACTICE WILL HELP YOU:

▶ Increase feelings of loving-kindness toward others.

▶ Increase awareness of the role of the mind and thoughts as a means to express loving-kindness.

▶ Expand your heart to embrace and extend loving-kindness to as many people as possible.

This is the last in the set of practices where we imagine lights extending out from ourselves that contain the ability to infuse others with the qualities of peace, love, and happiness. The first version pertained to the body and the actions of the body and worked with the imagery of white light extending out from the center of the head. The second version pertained to speech and the quality of speech and words and we worked with the imagery of red light extending out from the center of the throat. In this version we are going to imagine that we have a blue light that will come out from the center of our chests at the core of the body at the level of the heart that fills everyone it touches with peace, love, and happiness. As always we will envision that there is an endless source of this blue light and all those qualities within ourselves so there is no risk when we extend it out to other people of being depleted.

STEP ONE: Use the "First Invite Love In" meditation on page 15 before you begin this guided meditation.

STEP TWO: Please follow the instructions below for the central part of this compassion practice.

STEP THREE: Use the "Seal with a Vow and Rejoice" meditation on page 22 when you conclude this guided meditation.

1. Let's first locate the place in the center of your body where the blue light is envisioned to be coming from. Imagine you've got a channel running from the top of your head down through the center of your body. Now place your attention at the place in that channel that is at the level of your heart.

2. Visualize a beautiful, beautiful blue light radiating out from that spot that has the ability when it touches upon people to

light them up with feelings of peace, love, and happiness in their minds and their thoughts, such that all of their thoughts will have these qualities.

3. Now imagine that you can extend the light without any effort whatsoever. Visualize yourself extending the blue light a few inches around your body. Try that out.

4. Now effortlessly extend the light twenty or thirty feet. If you're inside, the light should be reaching through the walls to the outside of the building.

5. Next envision all the people in your neighborhood in a ten-block area.

6. Imagine the blue light comes out of you and touches upon all of the people in your neighborhood.

7. Imagine that when it touches upon them it causes their thoughts and their minds to be filled with feelings of peace, compassion, love, kindness, and happiness.

8. Now we will extend this visualization out to encompass the entire state. First see an area as large as your state and envision all the people in it.

9. Next imagine the blue light that carries with it feelings of peace, love, happiness, kindness, and compassion coming from your heart center, extending out, and touching upon all the people in your state.

10. See the blue light bringing their minds to a state of peace and happiness.

11. Now we're going to extend this visualization out to encompass the entire country and to reach to every person in the country. See the blue light extending out from your heart center and touching upon every single person in the country.

12. Imagine that when the blue light touches upon them it transforms their minds such that their minds are filled with feelings of peace, love, and happiness.

13. We'll finish by extending this exercise out to the entire planet in our minds. See the planet, the globe, a beautiful sphere hanging in space.

14. Envision all the people all over the planet.

15. See the blue light coming out from you without any effort. It just automatically extends out and has the ability when it

touches upon people to transform their minds so that they think peaceful, loving, happy, kind, and compassionate thoughts.

16. See the whole planet of people touched by this blue light, who have their minds and thoughts filled with love and peace. What a beautiful sight that would be!

 ## Short Form

Imagine a blue light in the center of your chest that sends out rays of love and peace in all directions. Imagine the light extends a few inches around your body. Continue extending the light until it encompasses your neighborhood, then your whole state, then your country, and finally until it bathes the entire earth in blue rays and everyone has a mind full of love and peace.

Thinking of All Living Beings
as Kind Mothers

THIS PRACTICE WILL HELP YOU:

▸ Expand your mind to the greatest extent possible
to embrace all living beings in the scope of your compassion
and loving-kindness.

▸ Increase trust of others by creating a sense of kinship.

▸ Increase love for others by creating a sense of gratitude.

▸ Reduce feelings of divisiveness and "us vs. them."

This is the last practice in the set based around the foundation practice of thinking of other living beings as having been your kindest, most loving, most ideal mother in an imagined past life. In this practice we are going to extend our vision of this to the broadest degree such that we imagine that every living being on the planet—human beings, animals, insects, birds, fish, invertebrates, every type of sentient being—has in an imagined past life been our kind mother to whom we would feel tremendous gratitude and love in return.

Step One: Use the "First Invite Love In" meditation on page 15 before you begin this guided meditation.

Step Two: Please follow the instructions below for the central part of this compassion practice.

Step Three: Use the "Seal with a Vow and Rejoice" meditation on page 22 when you conclude this guided meditation.

1. Begin by thinking about all the people in your neighborhood. Then think of all the animal life in the neighborhood—in the air, on the ground, under the ground, and in the water—including the very smallest life forms, little tiny mites and insects and anything else that's not a plant or rock. Try to get a sense of the magnitude of the living beings in your neighborhood.

2. Next imagine that every single one of these sentient beings has been your kindest, most loving, and caring mother in an imaginary past life. Imagine that they all took care of your every need. They were delighted when things went well for you and did everything they could do to make sure that your life was as good, safe, and happy as possible. They loved you

and comforted you when things didn't go well. Think that every single one of these living beings that you hold in your mind now has been such a kind mother in a past life.

3. Now imagine how grateful you would have felt in return for the love that all of these living beings in your neighborhood gave you. See in your mind's eye how much love you would have expressed back to them in those past lives. See the close bond between you with their care and love coming into you and your gratitude and love returning back out to them.

4. Next think of your state. Think of how many people are in your state. Get some sense of that in your mind. Then think of all the other kinds of living beings in the air, on the ground, living in the trees and bushes, underground, and in the water. Get a sense of the magnitude of all those kinds of living beings.

5. Now imagine that each and every one of them has been your kind mother in a past life. Get a sense of all those past lives and all those living beings having been your kind mother. Feel the love that you experienced and their care, protection, and support. See them rejoicing in the good things that happened in your life. Then feel yourself open up and feel so much gratitude and love in return to all these motherly living beings.

6. Next let's extend this imagery out to encompass the whole country. Sense the expanse of the country and all of the human beings in it. Sense the number of them and their distribution across the country. Now add into this visualization all other living beings in the country: in the air and water, underground, or on the ground.

7. Think that every single one of them has been your kind mother in an imagined past life. You are surrounded by hundreds of millions of living beings who had been the kindest mother to you an imaginary past life. Wow! That's a lot of love.

8. Imagine yourself in this close relationship with them and feeling great gratitude and love in return. See the love coming back out of you to them all because of the love, care, and support that came into you. Feel that for a moment.

9. Now think of the entire planet. See the whole globe, this orb of living beings, trillions of billions of them. There are unthinkable numbers of living beings on the planet—human beings and all other life forms. Get a sense of the magnitude of the mass of living beings on this planet.

10. Think that every single one of those beings has been the kindest mother in a past life for you. Imagine that they took

care of you in their bodies until you were born. Think that they took care of you kindly in your infancy, made sure you never went hungry, cleaned you, protected you, and did everything they could to make you happy. They rejoiced in your happiness and comforted you when things were tough. Imagine that they did everything they could to help you become strong and capable as you grew up. They looked upon you with loving eyes and held you with loving arms.

11. Now imagine that experience with all those living beings and feel the love that you would have felt in return and gratitude for having been so well taken care of in the imaginary past lives by the trillions of billions of living beings on this planet.

12. Visualize being surrounded and being on the planet with that much love, kindness, and compassion being exchanged back and forth. Hold that in your mind for as long as you can.

 SHORT FORM

Think about all the people and animals, including the smallest life forms, that live in your neighborhood. Imagine that in a past life all these people and animals have been the most loving and caring mothers to you conceivable. Imagine that all these made every sacrifice possible to shield you from danger, comfort you in sadness, and attend to your every need. Then think about how grateful you would have been to all these living beings when you were a child for taking such kind care of you. Now try this sequence thinking about all the people and animals in your state, then your country, and finally all the living beings on the entire earth.

Understanding the Role of Dualism as the Ultimate Source of Suffering

THIS PRACTICE WILL HELP YOU:

▶ Increase the power of your experience of loving-kindness by dissolving the dualistic mindset.

▶ Expand your mind to the greatest extent possible to embrace all living beings in compassion and loving-kindness.

▶ Increase trust of others by creating a sense of kinship.

▶ Increase love for others by creating a sense of gratitude.

▶ Reduce feelings of divisiveness and "us vs. them."

STEP ONE: Use the "First Invite Love In" meditation on page 15 before you begin this guided meditation.

STEP TWO: Please follow the instructions below for the central part of this compassion practice.

STEP THREE: Use the "Seal with a Vow and Rejoice" meditation on page 22 when you conclude this guided meditation.

A dualistic frame of mind can be thought of as the ultimate cause of all misery and suffering of human beings on the planet. Dualism causes people to put themselves before others, to put their own happiness before other people's happiness, and to make a distinction between "myself and my group" versus another person or another group. These views and distinctions lead to varying degrees of fear, anger, envy, pride, jealousy, selfishness, greed, and possessiveness. All of these feelings ultimately lead at the very least to personal unhappiness and at the worst to xenophobia, warfare, genocide, holocaust, and the like. You can view the dualistic frame of mind as the seed within every human being on the planet that will ripen into some sort of pain and suffering during their lifetimes.

1. Take a moment to envision the numbers of human beings on the planet and their distribution.

2. Then think that they have all been your kindest, most loving, and most caring mother in an imagined past life and that you in return feel tremendous gratitude and love toward each and every one of them.

3. Think that because of that love you would wish to spare them every possible pain and suffering that life might bring them.

4. Now imagine that all of these motherly human beings whom you wish to protect and for whom you wish only the best—imagine that all of them have within them the seeds of the dualistic mindset that is inevitably going to bring pain and suffering to them. They're either unaware of it or they're unable to do anything to get rid of it without some intervention. Without help they are going to suffer miserably sooner or later in their lives because of their dualistic mindset.

5. Feel your compassion to relieve them of suffering and desire to ensure that they have the most peaceful and happy life possible. Think that you wish that all human beings on the planet would have peaceful and happy lives guided by minds filled with love for all other human beings.

6. As your feeling of love, concern, and desire to protect all these motherly sentient beings rises up in you, imagine that it is expressed as a white light that comes out from your heart center and reaches out over the entire planet where it touches upon every single person and dissolves their dualistic mind frames. Imagine that it dissolves the core source of any future of unhappiness, pain, or suffering that they might experience. Take a minute to see that happening.

7. Next imagine that your feelings of compassion, love, and desire to free all these motherly sentient beings of pain and suffering become so great that your entire body, speech, and mind, your physical body, your thoughts, your spiritual essence, and your ethereal being dissolve into that white compassionate light, which causes it to spread even further and become even more powerful. Think that by dissolving into the compassionate white light you no longer exist as a separate distinct individual, but have become an element of compassion that is represented by white light within every motherly sentient being on the planet. Meditate on this for a few moments.

 ## Short Form

Visualize a white light in your heart that represents compassion. Imagine that this light increases and radiates out from you in all directions to reach all living beings. Then imagine that your own body, speech, and mind completely dissolve and transform into this white light. Now think that this light purifies all the dualistic thoughts of all living beings in the universe and fills them with peace and loving-kindness for all living beings. Meditate like this for as long as possible.

THE ULTIMATE COMPASSIONATE FORCE: DISSOLVING THE DUALISTIC MINDSET

THIS PRACTICE WILL HELP YOU:

▸ Increase the power of your experience of compassion
by dissolving the dualistic mindset.

▸ Create an association in your mind between a dualistic
mindset and the experience of suffering.

▸ Expand your mind to the greatest extent possible to embrace
all living beings in your compassion and loving-kindness.

▸ Increase trust of others by creating a sense of kinship.

▸ Increase love for others by creating a sense of gratitude.

▸ Reduce feelings of divisiveness and "us vs. them."

STEP ONE: Use the "First Invite Love In" meditation on page 15 before
you begin this guided meditation.

STEP TWO: Please follow the instructions below for the central part of this compassion practice.

STEP THREE: Use the "Seal with a Vow and Rejoice" meditation on page 22 when you conclude this guided meditation.

1. Begin by thinking of all the living beings all over the planet. Get a sense of the great magnitude of these. Perhaps you can see them as points of light all over the planet.

2. Think that every last one of these living beings has been the kindest and most caring, loving mother to you in an imaginary past life.

3. See and feel the love that came into you. Imagine the years and years of care, nurturing, protection, and support, the rejoicing and happiness. Feel what it would have been like to be loved in that fashion.

4. Feel all the gratitude and love that would have come out of you in return to all of these motherly sentient beings all over the planet. Feel a great sense of love and compassion for every single sentient being on the planet.

5. Now contemplate the fact that at some point during the course of their lives every single one of these motherly sentient

beings will experience some illness, disease, or other type of obstacle or obstruction to their happiness and their health.

6. Feel the concern that you would have for all these motherly sentient beings who have been so kind to you in an imagined past life and how much you would wish to relieve them of that suffering in return.

7. Let that feeling of compassion and desire to relieve them of the suffering of illness and obstructions to their peace and health and happiness rise up inside you. Allow it to well up and become stronger and then imagine that it manifests as a red light coming from an unending source of healing power within you. Imagine that this light has the ability to cure illnesses and diseases and to purify and eliminate obstacles to health and happiness.

8. Visualize this red light extending out from you with no effort on your part. It automatically extends out to all the sentient beings who have been such kind mothers to you in past lives and cures their illnesses so that they completely are freed from the possibility of suffering. It eliminates and purifies any obstacles or obstructions to their health or happiness such that their future will be healthy and free of suffering of all kinds. Just imagine that.

9. Now imagine that your compassion for all of these motherly sentient beings and your desire to relieve them of any possible suffering from illness or obstructions in their lives becomes greater and greater. Imagine that, in order to give full power to your intention and desire to extend your compassion to these beings, your body, speech, mind, and all of the physical aspects of your body as well as your thoughts, your feelings, your spiritual essence, and your ethereal being—every last element of something that could be identified as you, separate and apart from all other beings—dissolve into the red light that is radiating out to all motherly sentient beings as a healing force.

10. Take some time to meditate on the imagery of dissolving completely into the compassionate impulse, radiating out along the rays of red compassionate light, and being distributed as points of red healing light within each and every motherly sentient being on the planet.

 Short Form

Visualize all the living beings who are suffering with disease and obstructions in their lives. Now imagine a red light in your heart that has the power to cure sick people and purify them of their disease and obstructions. Imagine that this light increases and radiates in all directions to reach all living beings. Then imagine that your own body, speech, and mind completely dissolve and transform into this healing and purifying red light, which reaches all living beings in the universe and causes them to recover from their illnesses and experience peace and happiness. Meditate like this for as long as possible.

Afterword

What a wonderful thing you have accomplished by opening your heart in this way! For what could be more essential as a way to secure your own happiness and to contribute to making this world a better place to live in harmoniously together than to take steps, as you have, to develop a more loving and peaceful mind?

One thought leads to a million others over time. Now, you have at hand a technique that with time and practice will create a bulwark against the negative thought patterns built up through a lifetime of experience; a technique that will end mental patterns that can lead to galaxies of painful and energy-draining thoughts. Now, you have begun to create a safe haven, a place in your mind to rest, enjoy, and envision yourself within a loving universe.

Just imagine the positive ripple effect in the world as you interact with others in a kinder and more peaceful manner. Think of how many people you catch a glimpse of each day and interact with in small, seemingly inconsequential ways. A kinder word or look from you will surely register in their minds and feelings. And this will lead in some measure to some softening of their views and warming of their reactions to others who, in turn, will respond in a gentler, kinder way to other people. Consider the multiplier effect over time of your more compassionate and peaceful heart. Consider the numbers of people transferring the mote of happiness onward that they received from their encounter with you. It is a world of phenomenal good you have set in motion.

On a more intimate plane, the impact of your attainment of a happier and more peaceful mind on close friends, family members, and co-workers may be more striking and far reaching. How wonderful. How good!

So, this is a good beginning that you have made in training for a more compassionate and peaceful mind, though surely not an end or final achievement. Reading these practices and understanding them intellectually can produce a valuable effect—if a superficial and fleeting one. Visualizing them once or twice will deepen your understanding, but the effect on your life and state of mind will still be transitory. When getting in shape physically there is no letting up once one has achieved a healthy and strong body; in the same way, you must continually work the peace muscles of your mind, as it were, to hold and protect the safe haven of love and peace that you have begun to build. Without constant daily effort on your part to maintain and restore the bulwarks of these new healthier and happier ways of thinking and feeling, the waves of old thought patterns will erode this haven like the walls of a sandcastle.

So please, do find a way to work with these practices daily and to incorporate them into your way of life. There are greater depths of understanding to be achieved, and with each fresh round of effort, more profound states of relaxation and pleasure to be experienced. All this awaits you.

Make this way of thinking your way of life and your constant goal and view. Give yourself the gift of time every day to renew yourself and commit to serving as a pillar of love, compassion, and understanding for our companions as we go through life together on this, our dear earth.

You can do it. You are doing it! How wonderful!

APPENDIX:

Full Set of Short Forms of Compassion Practices

The following is a complete list of all of the short forms of compassion practices, compiled here for your easy reference as you become more comfortable with the meditations. Although the opening "First Invite Love In" and closing "Seal with a Vow and Rejoice" meditations are not listed as part of each exercise here, please make sure to diligently begin and end each time with them, as they will sustain your practice.

 FIRST INVITE LOVE IN

Bring to mind your spiritual support figure. Feel their unconditional love beaming into you with perfect concentration for as long as you need. Ask for their help in transforming your mind and see them respond joyfully and happy to help. Aspire to a mind of greater compassion and kindness. Clear your mind and body of distraction, tension, desire, and aversion. Shift your point of perception to your third eye and imagine that you can see and receive your spiritual support figure's state of mind through that portal. Think that your spiritual support figure performs a high-level version of whatever compassion practice you are following, in order to support you.

 ## Seal with a Vow and Rejoice

Imagine your spiritual support figure is pleased with your compassion practice. Vow to continue your efforts. Visualize your support figure and all the compassionate thoughts you generated transforming into two pea-sized balls of light. Imagine these two balls coming down from the crown of your head to rest in a flower of light at your heart center. Imagine the petals closing around them to store and protect them. Be kind and patient with yourself.

1. Thinking of Friends as Kind Mothers

Think about a friend or someone you like very much. Imagine that in a past life this person had been the most loving and caring mother to you conceivable. Imagine that this person made every sacrifice possible to shield you from danger, comfort you in sadness, and attend to your every need. Then think about how grateful you would have been to this person when they were taking such kind care of you when you were a child. Now try this in your mind as much as possible, thinking about other people you like or consider as friends.

2. Breathe In with Compassion, Breathe Out with Loving-Kindness (Part 1)

Imagine that you have the power to relieve all the misery and suffering of all living beings by first breathing it like harmless black smoke or mist into yourself. Then imagine that from your store of merit and virtue, built up from the good things you have done and thought during your life, you send out peace and happiness to all living beings by infusing them with inexhaustible brilliant white light as you breathe out. Repeat this as many times as possible.

3. Widening the Heart to Embrace the World with Loving-Kindness and Rejoicing

Imagine all the wonderful things you hope will happen in the life of someone you care deeply about. Imagine their happiness when these things take place. Next imagine that this happens to every person in your family. Then to all of your friends. Then to everyone in your neighborhood, your state, your country, and ultimately to everyone in the world.

4. Bearing Compassionate Witness to Suffering (Part 1)

Imagine you have a child who fell into a swift river and is being carried away to certain death by drowning. Your child cries out to you to save him. Imagine that you have no arms and that you are running along the banks of the river, unable to save your child. There is no help in sight and nothing you can do to prevent your child, who is looking into your eyes with fear and desperation, from drowning soon.

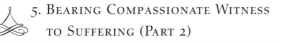

5. Bearing Compassionate Witness to Suffering (Part 2)

Think of a place in the world that is war torn. Imagine yourself as a mother there finding out that one of her children has suffered a serious injury that will make it impossible for them to lead a normal life again. Imagine your sadness upon seeing your child with a missing limb, loss of sight, or loss of motion or mental ability. If possible, think about this in every place in the world where there is war now.

6. Bearing Compassionate Witness to Suffering (Part 3)

Imagine a place in the world where people are starving. Imagine yourself as a mother of a beloved child who is starving to death in your arms because you cannot find food to feed her. Imagine there is no possible hope of finding food before the child dies. Look into the child's eyes and see the suffering that you can do nothing to relieve. If possible, think about this in every place in the world where people are now starving to death.

7. Widening the Heart to Embrace the World with Loving-Kindness (Sunshine Metaphor)

Imagine that when the sun shines brightly its rays are full of love and peace, which enter the minds and bodies of someone you love dearly, filling them with happiness, peace, strength, and hope. Then imagine this happens to every person in your family when they stand in sunlight. Then to all of your friends. Then to everyone in your neighborhood, your state, your country, and ultimately to everyone in the world.

8. Overcoming Anger and Bitterness with Compassion

Think of someone who annoys you or whom you don't like. Think about something in their lives that is causing them to be unhappy. Imagine how sad and upset they are about this situation. Then imagine that you give them what they need to be happy or stop whatever is happening that is now making them unhappy. Imagine how peaceful and happy they feel now that their lives are better.

9. Widening the Heart to Embrace the World with Loving-Kindness (Snowfall Metaphor)

Imagine a day when snow is falling in light fluffy flakes. Imagine that each flake is filled with a substance that brings complete and utter joy and happiness to living beings. Imagine that endless snowflakes fall onto someone you love and dissolve into them, filling them with inconceivable joy and happiness. Then imagine this happens to all of your friends and every person in your family. Then to everyone in your neighborhood, your state, your country, and ultimately to everyone in the world.

10. Taking Compassion into Daily Life: Feeling Compassion for Strangers

Look carefully at a stranger. Try to imagine what makes this person unhappy in their life. Then imagine that you could change this person's life so that they have whatever they need to be happy. Think about this person feeling very happy and peaceful. Now try this with as many strangers as possible.

11. Increasing Generosity by Imagining Helping Others During a Famine

Imagine that there has been a great famine and there is widespread terrible suffering and starvation. There is no food to be found anywhere, but you have miraculously unending stores of highly nutritious food in your house. Imagine the doorbell rings and someone who is starving asks you for food. Visualize handing out lifesaving food to one visitor after another, each of whom weeps with relief and gratitude. Do this for as long as you can.

12. Taking Compassion into Daily Life: Imagining Strangers as Kind Mothers

Look carefully at the face of a complete stranger. Imagine that in a past life this person had been the most loving and caring mother to you conceivable. Imagine that this person made every sacrifice possible to shield you from danger, comfort you in sadness, and attend to your every need. Then think about how grateful you would have been to this person when they were taking such kind care of you when you were a child. Now try this with as many strangers as possible.

13. Connecting the Body and Actions with Compassion

Imagine a white light in the center of your head that sends out rays of love and peace in all directions. Imagine the white light extends a few inches around your body. Continue extending the light until it encompasses your neighborhood, then your whole state, then your country, and finally until it bathes the entire earth in white rays and everyone on earth acts out of love and peace.

14. Increasing Generosity by Imagining Giving All to Save the Life of a Loved One

Imagine that someone you love very dearly will die if they do not receive a lifesaving operation very soon. They don't have the money to pay for the operation and neither do you. The only way you can save this loved one's life is to clear out your bank account and sell all of your assets to pay for the operation. Visualize going to the bank to get the money, doing whatever is necessary to sell all of your assets, and giving the money to the person. Visualize the person's relief and happiness to know they will have the funds to pay for their lifesaving operation.

15. Opening the Heart by Loosening the Grip of Possessiveness

Think of the five favorite objects you own. Next imagine each object has a substance that will save the life of the five people in your life whom you care most deeply about. For some reason, each person will definitely die if you do not give them one of your prized possessions. Now imagine that you give away permanently and irreversibly the object to the person. Next visualize how relieved and grateful they are as they walk away with the object. Then if you can, imagine that there are hundreds of people whose lives are in danger and that one by one you give away everything you own in order to save their lives.

16. Widening the Heart to Embrace the World with Loving-Kindness (Song Metaphor)

Imagine that you can sing a song that is so exquisite that it brings indescribable happiness to everyone who hears it. Imagine that when someone hears this song they, too, start singing in the same way. First sing the song to everyone you care deeply about, then to people you don't like, then to a stadium full of strangers, then to a vast expanse of people as far as the eye can see. Remember to imagine hearing everyone singing the song after you first sing it to them.

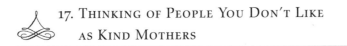

17. Thinking of People You Don't Like as Kind Mothers

Think about someone who has upset, irritated, or angered you. Imagine that in a past life this person had been the most loving and caring mother to you conceivable. Imagine that this person made every sacrifice possible to shield you from danger, comfort you in sadness, and attend to your every need. Then think about how grateful you would have been to this person when they were taking such kind care of you when you were a child. Now try this with as many people as possible who have upset, hurt, or angered you in the past.

18. Increasing Loving-Kindness by Rejoicing for the Good Fortune of Others (Happiness Version)

Think of someone you like a lot and imagine that their life takes a miraculous turn for the good and they are blessed with great health, wealth, and success of every kind. Imagine yourself being happy for them without any trace of jealousy, bitterness, or envy. Next think of someone who at some point in your life did something mean or unkind to you that had really upset you. Now imagine that their lives take a miraculous turn for the good and they too are blessed with great health, wealth, and success of every kind. Imagine yourself being happy for them without any trace of jealousy, bitterness, or envy.

19. Reducing Pride and Egotism through Remorse

Think of someone to whom you have been unkind or unfair at some point in your life. Imagine going to the person and apologizing profusely and sincerely for what you did and that this act of contrition completely heals the hurt or angry feelings they have harbored in their minds. Imagine everyone in the world going to people whom they have hurt or been unkind or unfair to and doing the same thing with the same healing results.

20. INCREASING LOVING-KINDNESS BY REJOICING FOR THE GOOD FORTUNE OF OTHERS (WEALTH VERSION)

Imagine that everyone you know suddenly comes into great wealth. Think of this person by person with joy for their good fortune and without any trace of jealousy, bitterness, or envy. Now imagine that great wealth comes to everyone in your neighborhood, your state, your country, and ultimately to everyone in the world.

21. TAKING COMPASSION INTO DAILY LIFE: SPEAKING TO STRANGERS WITH LOVING-KINDNESS

Imagine that your voice and words carry the power of love in them. Before you talk to someone, have the intention in your mind that, no matter what it is that you say, somehow your words will have a peaceful, soothing, and beneficial effect on the person. Try this with a stranger, perhaps at a checkout counter at a store. Do this as much as possible.

22. Imagining Others Are Cleansed of the Source of Suffering

Think of someone you care deeply about and imagine that the person is surrounded by a field of white light that has the miraculous power to cleanse negativity in all forms. Imagine that all the pores in this person's body open up and that the cleansing white light enters their body, washing away all the mental effects of everything negative that has been done to them or that they have done to others. The negativity comes out of their pores and their lower orifices as soot or gray mist leaving this person with a mental state of peace, clarity, love, and joy. The pores then close to seal in and protect the purity of this person's state of mind. Next imagine this sequence happening to all of your friends and every person in your family. Then to everyone in your neighborhood, your state, your country, and ultimately to everyone in the world.

23. Taking the Practice of Compassion into Daily Life: Looking at Strangers with Loving-Kindness

Look a stranger in the eyes, think that they had once been your kind mother, and smile warmly at them. Do this with as many strangers as possible.

24. Bearing Compassionate Witness to Suffering (Part 4)

Think of someplace in the world where you know that animals are having trouble finding enough food to survive. Imagine an animal too exhausted to search any more for food, stumbling to the ground and trying unsuccessfully to rise again. Imagine the days it lies there, thirsty and suffering from terrible hunger, until it succumbs to death. Imagine how helpless and hopeless it feels. Now think about the actual number of animals in this area that are suffering in this way. If you can, think about other places in the world and other kinds of animals that are also starving to death.

25. Connecting the Voice and Speech with Compassion

Imagine a red light in the center of your throat that sends out rays of love and peace in all directions. Imagine the red light extends a few inches around your body. Continue extending the light until it encompasses your neighborhood, then your whole state, then your country, and finally until it bathes the entire earth in red rays and everyone on earth speaks from a place of love and peace.

26. Thinking of Animals as Kind Mothers

Think about a particular animal you know and like. Imagine that in a past life this animal had been the most loving and caring mother to you conceivable. Imagine that this animal made every sacrifice possible to shield you from danger, comfort you in sadness, and attend to your every need. Then think about how grateful you would have been when you were a child to this animal for taking such kind care of you. Now try this sequence thinking about all the animals, including the smallest life forms, in your neighborhood, state, then your country, and finally throughout the entire earth.

FIRST INVITE
LOVE IN

230

27. Imagining Sharing the Source of Your Good Fortune with Others

Imagine you could take the source of all of your past and future good fortune—the source of all your health, success, money, happiness, and peace of mind—and make a replica of it that you put in box. Now imagine giving this box to your mother so that she will have good fortune. Then to your father, to the rest of your family and friends, to people you don't like, to everyone in your neighborhood, your state, your country, and ultimately to everyone in the world.

28. Breathe In with Compassion, Breathe Out with Loving-Kindness (Part 2)

Imagine that you have the power to relieve people of the mental suffering they experience as a result of the cruel and unkind things that have been done to them. Imagine that you can take away the memory and impact of those terrible experiences by breathing them into yourself in the form of black smoke or mist. Then imagine that, from your store of merit and virtue built up from the good things you have done and thought during your life, you send out peace and happiness to all living beings by infusing them with brilliant white light as you breathe out. Repeat this as many times as possible.

29. Expanding the Heart to Have Compassion for People Who Have Been Unfair or Hurt You

Think about someone who has done an injustice to you that still makes you hurt or angry when you think about it. Then imagine the negativity that is in this person's mind and the ways that this negativity is hurting their chance to have a happy and peaceful life. Now imagine that you can take this negativity out of their mindstream and replace it with compassion and loving-kindness. If you can, think this way about each and every person you feel has acted badly toward you.

30. Bearing Compassionate Witness to Suffering (Part 5)

Think about a place in the world where animals are badly mistreated by people who use them for labor. Think about a particular beast of burden that is worn out and too tired to do what its master wants no matter how hard it tries. Then think about the animal being harshly yelled at and beaten until its skin is cut and it bleeds. Now multiply this situation by the number of animals you think are probably suffering like that in this place at this very moment. Then if you can, think about animals in other parts of the world that are suffering terribly in the same way with no hope of relief except their death.

31. Taking Compassion into Daily Life: Imagining Generosity toward Strangers

Look at a stranger and imagine giving them everything you own: the keys to your home, your car, all your belongings, and all your money and assets. Think like this for as many strangers as possible. (It won't hurt you to just imagine this. It doesn't cost you anything really. It is the thought that counts, but it is surprisingly hard to entertain this idea as a thought even though it has no real consequences.)

32. Overcoming Jealousy and Envy to Rejoice for the Emotional Happiness of Others

Think about someone you know who feels lonely and experiences a lot of pain and sadness because they wish they had a loving partner in their lives. Now imagine that someone kind and wonderful comes into their lives, someone who immediately loves them deeply and wants to spend the rest of their lives together with them. Imagine the love, joy, and bliss this person feels now that they experience a deep and secure love. Imagine this happens to all the lonely people you know. Then it happens to all the lonely people in your neighborhood, state, country, and the world.

33. Taking Compassion into Daily Life: Imbuing Simple Greetings with Compassion

Look for someone on the street or in a public place who seems sad, hurt, or upset. Look them in the eyes, smile warmly at them, and wish them a good day. Do this for as many people as possible.

34. Bearing Compassionate Witness to Suffering (Part 6)

Look at a bird or a squirrel living outside. Think about what its life is like. Think about how it has to find food every day. Think about it trying to find shelter when it is cold, windy, and raining or snowing. Think about how other animals chase it away from food it needs and the place where it wants to rest. Think about how it will eventually die through accident, being attacked by other animals, through sickness, or starvation. Do this for as many animals as possible.

35. Transforming Our Own Suffering into a Compassionate Impulse

Think about something sad that has happened in your life. Now imagine that, by virtue of your having experienced that sad event, you could prevent any other person on earth from ever having to experience the same kind of unfortunate event. Imagine this first with regard to people you care deeply about. Then imagine you could save people you don't like from suffering in this way.

36. Breathe In with Compassion, Breathe Out with Loving-Kindness (Part 3)

Imagine that you have the power to relieve people of the negativity they have created in their minds as a result of having thought, said, or done cruel or unkind things to other people.

Imagine that you can take away the memory and impact of those negative thoughts, words, and actions by breathing them into yourself in the form of black smoke or mist. Then imagine that, from your store of merit and virtue built up from the good things you have done and thought during your life, you send out peace and happiness to all living beings by infusing them with brilliant white light as you breathe out. Repeat this as many times as possible.

37. Connecting the Mind and Thoughts with Compassion

Imagine a blue light in the center of your chest that sends out rays of love and peace in all directions. Imagine the light extends a few inches around your body. Continue extending the light until it encompasses your neighborhood, then your whole state, then your country, and finally until it bathes the entire earth in blue rays and everyone has a mind full of love and peace.

38. Thinking of All Living Beings as Kind Mothers

Think about all the people and animals, including the smallest life forms, that live in your neighborhood. Imagine that in a past life all these people and animals have been the most loving and caring mothers to you conceivable. Imagine that all these made every sacrifice possible to shield you from danger, comfort you in sadness, and attend to your every need. Then think about how grateful you would have been to all these living beings when you were a child for taking such kind care of you. Now try this sequence thinking about all the people and animals in your state, then your country, and finally all the living beings on the entire earth.

39. Understanding the Role of Dualism as the Ultimate Source of Suffering

Visualize a white light in your heart that represents compassion. Imagine that this light increases and radiates out from you in all directions to reach all living beings. Then imagine that your own body, speech, and mind completely dissolve and transform into this white light. Now think that this light purifies all the dualistic thoughts of all living beings in the universe and fills them with peace and loving-kindness for all living beings. Meditate like this for as long as possible.

40. The Ultimate Compassionate Force: Dissolving the Dualistic Mindset

Visualize all the living beings who are suffering with disease and obstructions in their lives. Now imagine a red light in your heart that has the power to cure sick people and purify them of their disease and obstructions. Imagine that this light increases and radiates in all directions to reach all living beings. Then imagine that your own body, speech, and mind completely dissolve and transform into this healing and purifying red light, which reaches all living beings in the universe and causes them to recover from their illnesses and experience peace and happiness. Meditate like this for as long as possible.

ACKNOWLEDGMENTS

His Holiness Penor Rinpoche hoped that the precious techniques in this book would reach and benefit a vast audience of people who would not otherwise have had access to them. To my mind, I am not the author of this book, but merely the vehicle to provide a cultural translation of the precious and powerful compassion practices he taught and lived. As such, I will do everything in my power to fulfill all of Penor Rinpoche's most noble and kind aspirations for the benefit of this book.

This book would never have come into being were it not for the insights and support of three people: Lama Lobsang Chophel, Josh Bartok, and John Hamilton. Upon reading the original short descriptions of the core practices Lama Lobsang, H.H. Penor Rinpoche's secretary for thirty years, recognized it as consistent with and a contemporary expression of Dharma and immediately brought it to His Holiness' attention. From that point on until the present day, Lama Lobsang has done everything possible to bring the book to light for the benefit of all beings. His vision and keen insight have been as a lodestar for me, wisely and kindly guiding me at every juncture along the way.

Josh Bartok, my extraordinary editor, saw the elements of a full book in the glimmer of a few short pages, and with wizardly deft direction led me step by step, and year by year, along a path which resulted in a form of presentation I never envisioned, but which suits and serves perfectly for its purposes and audience. His kindness in times of despair and calm fairness in times of pique (sorry!) kept me in check and on track. There can be no better editor or friend than Josh.

John Hamilton, my dear friend and spiritual companion of many years, surprised me with generous financial help when none was sought or expected, but came at the perfect time to provide me a broad expanse of time to expand on the core practices and make full guided meditations of them all. Without the peace of mind his generous gift afforded, I doubt that I could have found the composure required to allow the details of the meditations to surface clearly and fully in my mind.

In addition, I would like to express my appreciation to the following people for their contributions to bringing this book to light: my son, Chris Edley; my parents, Al Pesso and Diane Boyden-Pesso; my sister, Tasmin Pesso; Master Yan Xin for the inspiration for some of the visualization techniques incorporated into the main meditation; Konchog Norbu for being the best Dharma friend possible and a very savvy and helpful editor; Tim McNeill of Wisdom Publications for supporting this project, and Laura Cunningham of Wisdom for all her efforts to improve the manuscript; Zaida Coles Edley, my godmother, for her shower of love and constant warm embrace; Diane Garthwaite for generous support in the early days; Ngodup Dorji of Shingkhar Ling, and Khenpo Nyima Dondrub for friendship and translating the text into Tibetan for Penor Rinpoche; Thinley Tenzin, my godson, for taking care of me so kindly during my visit at Namdroling Monastery to confer with Penor Rinpoche about the core practices; Tulku Ajam Rinpoche for carefully reviewing every idea and word of the near final draft; Kelly Nezat for his generous heart and support; and all my friends for their cheery encouragement throughout the long years of bringing this book to fruition.

Last, but not least, I would like to thank H.E. Tulku Ogyen Gyurmed Wanggyal Rinpoche from the bottom of my heart for appearing at this moment in time to kindly lend his support and serve as a bridge to and conduit for the blessings of our root guru, His Holiness Penor Rinpoche, as we go forth in the coming months and years to bring the joyous and healing message of the book to the world.

About the Authors

 Tana Pesso holds an undergraduate degree from Harvard College and a master's degree in public policy from the Kennedy School of Government, Harvard University. She lives in Rockport, MA.

Penor Rinpoche was the head of the Nyingma school of Tibetan Buddhism. Born in 1932 in Eastern Tibet he was renowned by all as an exemplary master of the Tibetan tradition. He tirelessly taught devoted students around the world. He passed away in 2009.

About Wisdom Publications

Wisdom Publications, a nonprofit publisher, is dedicated to making available authentic works relating to Buddhism for the benefit of all. We publish books by ancient and modern masters in all traditions of Buddhism, translations of important texts, and original scholarship. Additionally, we offer books that explore East-West themes unfolding as traditional Buddhism encounters our modern culture in all its aspects. Our titles are published with the appreciation of Buddhism as a living philosophy, and with the special commitment to preserve and transmit important works from Buddhism's many traditions.

To learn more about Wisdom, or to browse books online, visit our website at www.wisdompubs.org.

You may request a copy of our catalog online
or by writing to this address:

WISDOM PUBLICATIONS
199 Elm Street
Somerville, Massachusetts 02144 USA
Telephone: 617-776-7416
Fax: 617-776-7841
Email: info@wisdompubs.org
www.wisdompubs.org

THE WISDOM TRUST

As a nonprofit publisher, Wisdom is dedicated to the publication of Dharma books for the benefit of all sentient beings and dependent upon the kindness and generosity of sponsors in order to do so. If you would like to make a donation to Wisdom, you may do so through our website or our Somerville office. If you would like to help sponsor the publication of a book, please write or email us at the address above.

Thank you.